THE
NEVER-BE-BORED
★ ★ ★ BOOK ★ ★ ★

THE
NEVER-BE-BORED
BOOK ★ ★ ★

★ ★ ★

· · · · · · ·

Quick Things to Make
When There's Nothing to Do
Judith Logan Lehne

· ·

Illustrated by Morissa Lipstein

Sterling Publishing Co., Inc.   New York

Edited by Jeanette Green

Library of Congress Cataloging-in-Publication Data

Lehne, Judith Logan.
The Never-be-bored book : quick things to make when there's nothing to do / by Judith Logan Lehne ; illustrated by Morissa Lipstein.
p. cm.
Summary: Includes instructions, and in some cases background information, for a variety of artistic or useful items that can be made with readily available materials.
Includes index.
ISBN 0-8069-1254-5
1. Handicraft—Juvenile literature. [1. Handicraft.]
I. Lipstein, Morissa, ill. II. Title.
TT160.L445   1992
745.5—dc20   92-16529
                                               CIP
                                                AC

Several projects in this volume previously appeared in altered form in *Children's Albumn* magazine.

2   4   6   8   10   9   7   5   3   1

First paperback edition published in 1994 by
Sterling Publishing Company, Inc.
387 Park Avenue South, New York, N.Y. 10016
© 1992 by Judith Logan Lehne
Distributed in Canada by Sterling Publishing
% Canadian Manda Group, P.O. Box 920, Station U
Toronto, Ontario, Canada M8Z 5P9
Distributed in Great Britain and Europe by Cassell PLC
Villiers House, 41/47 Strand, London WC2N 5JE, England
Distributed in Australia by Capricorn Link (Australia) Pty Ltd.
P.O. Box 6651, Baulkham Hills, Business Centre, NSW 2153, Australia
Manufactured in the United States of America

Sterling ISBN 0-8069-1254-5 Trade
0-8069-1255-3 Paper

To my children, Shane, Kyle, Todd, and Tessa,
for sharing their imagination with me,
giving me an excuse to play, and keeping
the spirit of childhood alive in our home

Acknowledgments

Many of the projects presented in this book came from friends and teachers I've worked with both as a child and as an adult. Thanks to all of you for sharing your creativity with me and helping me to take flight on my own creative wings.

Special thanks to my husband, Ed, who endured (among other things!) scraps of this and globs of that around the house while I worked out countless craft projects. And thanks, too, for teaching me about the eagle!

Thanks also to Mary Anne for diligent assistance with the preliminary preparations and to Morissa for sticking with me all the way.

To Debby, Patty, Rich and Greg: Thanks for believing in me and for showing me how to believe in myself.

Contents

PROJECTS WITH STYLE

RECIPE FILE

Introduction

You say you're bored with baseball
  on a hot summer day?
You say the autumn wind
  has blown the blahs your way?
You say the springtime rain
  has dampened all your fun?
And winter feels like it'll last
  until you're twenty-one?
Say no more! Don't whine and cry!
Boredom's a thing of the past!
With imagination and a few supplies,
You can still have a blast!

Whether you're looking for a way to get rid of the "nothing-to-do's"—which attack us all some-time—or need a gift for a friend or a project idea for school, you'll find just what you need in this book. These projects are not "busy work," the kinds of things you make and throw away. Each activity allows you to create *real* artwork and things you can use every day. You also get a chance to learn about different cultures since you make replicas of traditional objects, artworks, and musical instruments. And you can engage in simple scientific experiments. But, most of all, you'll have a terrific time.

You will be able to work on most projects and activities alone or with friends. But some projects require the use of sharp knives or hot stoves, so be sure to ask an adult to read the directions with you before you begin. You'll find the easier, quick projects—which take from minutes to one day—in the first section of the book. More complicated projects are in the second section. But don't shy away from these more difficult crafts. If you're patient, you will be rewarded with a wonderful finished product.

Since many of us search for ways to make spending money, this book includes projects that you could sell at arts and crafts fairs or garage sales. And, of course, you can make lovely, inexpensive gifts for friends, family, and teachers. Most materials for these craft projects can be found in nature or in your own home. You can buy other materials for very little.

So, close the door on your boredom, and open yourself up to the magic world of creativity and imagination. I hope you'll have a little serendipity—finding happy surprises—and lots of enjoyment in these pages.

Judith Logan Lehne

Preparations

Since boredom often takes us by surprise, it's best to be prepared with lots of things to ward it off. In each of these projects, needed materials are listed separately from the directions. Most materials can be commonly found in nature or around the house. Others can be found at arts and crafts shops, variety stores, or hardware stores.

HERE'S WHAT TO DO

- Read the lists of materials for several projects that interest you, and gather the materials to keep in your Never-Be-Bored Box.

- Read all directions for the project you choose *before* beginning. If, for instance, the project requires that you use a recipe in the book's Recipe File (pp. 101–122), read those instructions, too.

- If you'll need a little help, ask an adult to read the project directions, too. Projects that require the use of stoves, ovens, knives, or sharp tools are preceded by a Helping Hands symbol, followed by a HOT! or SHARP! symbol.

HELPING HANDS　　**HOT!**　　**SHARP!**

- Prepare your work surface with newspapers or plastic so that it will be protected.

- Set out all ingredients or materials first. This also helps you see that you've got everything you'll need.

- Then follow all directions—step-by-step—very carefully.

- Have fun!

CRAFTS QUICK TO PLEASE

make them with ease

Dream Catchers

These pretty homemade webs are adapted from the American Indian culture. According to Indian lore, if a child hangs a Dream Catcher over the bed, the web will "catch" the bad dreams and let the good dreams through. Do you know someone who could use a Dream Catcher?

YOU'LL NEED

forked twig, *green*, not dry
2 to 3 yards of yarn or string
white liquid glue
feathers or beads
scissors

DIRECTIONS

1. Bring the forked ends of the twig together, and wind the yarn or string in a crisscross way to hold the ends in place. Knot the yarn, and let 4 to 6 inches of yarn hang down.

2. Begin where you've tied the twig branches together. Tie four separate pieces of yarn across the opening of the twig branches to create a wheel-spoke pattern. Knot each end of yarn as you work.

3. As you draw the fourth piece of yarn across the opening, wind the strand around the yarns at the center once or twice. Then pull the strand to the other side and knot it.

4. Snip off the excess yarn ends close to each knot.

5. Put several drops of glue on each crossed strand so that you create a spiral of glue dots.

6. With a long piece of yarn, set the yarn onto each glue spot, connecting the dots until you've created a "web." Press

each spot with your finger to help the yarn strands adhere to each other.

7. When the glue is dry, attach beads or feathers to the hanging strands of yarn at the bottom of the Dream Catcher.

8. Make a yarn bow at the top. Add more beads if you wish.

Then, off to bed to enjoy sweet dreams!

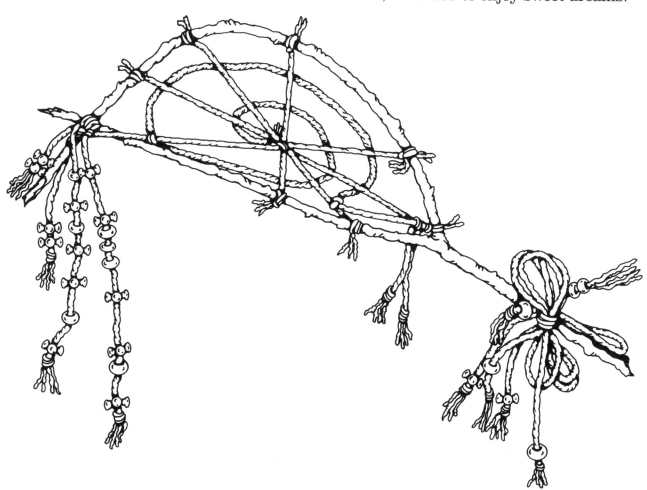

19

Hullabaloo Kazoo

YOU'LL NEED

6-inch cardboard tube
4-inch square of cellophane or
    waxed paper
rubber band
medley of tunes

★ ★ ★ ★ ★ ★ ★ ★

DIRECTIONS

1. Cut a cardboard tube so that it's 6 inches long, or use an empty toilet tissue roll.

2. Spread the cellophane or waxed paper square over one end of the tube. (Do not use plastic wrap.)

3. Secure the paper with a rubber band.

Place the *open end* of the tube against your mouth and hum. You may have to experiment with different mouth positions before the kazoo will distort the sound of your voice.

Make several kazoos, and invite your friends to form a Hullabaloo Kazoo Band.

If you wish, you could also decorate your kazoo by painting it or adding decals. Just avoid painting the mouthpiece, since most paints are inedible!

Blizzard in a Jar

Imagine snow swirling around tiny trees, miniature animals, or soldiers—even on a hot summer day. With a few ingredients, you can create a snowstorm to keep in your room all year long.

YOU'LL NEED

small jar
moth flakes, glitter, or crayon
    shavings
water
waterproof glue
small plastic or glass figures

DIRECTIONS

1. Glue the glass or plastic figures to the inside bottom of the jar. Allow them to dry for 24 hours.

2. Fill the jar with water, leaving a ½-inch space at the top.

3. Add 2 tablespoons of moth flakes for white snow. Or you can make snow in different colors with glitter or crayon shavings.

4. Coat the rim of the lid with glue. Screw the lid on the jar, and allow the glue to dry.

Shake the jar and turn it upside down. When you turn the jar upright, you'll see a blizzard.

Paper Fortune-Teller

With a quick lesson in paper folding, you'll soon be able to "predict" the future for your friends. Or you'll be able to create a Smile-Maker that coaxes your parents to smile.

YOU'LL NEED

8½-by-8½-inch square of
    white paper
pen or pencil
pocketful of dreams

PAPER FOLDING

1. With the paper square flat, fold all four corners in so that they meet at the center. You may use a larger or smaller square of paper, but this 8½-inch square works nicely.

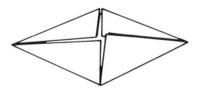

2. Turn the paper over, and again fold corners to meet in the center.

3. Turn the paper again, and fold it in half, corner to corner. Reopen it.

4. Fold the other two corners together.

5. Reopen the paper form with the four square flaps up.

6. Stick your index fingers and thumbs under the four flaps, and move the Paper Fortune-Teller back and forth and side to side.

TELLING FORTUNES

1. Fold the Paper Fortune-Teller again so that you can place your fingers under the flaps.

2. Ask a friend to pick one of the four numbers that are showing.

3. Work the Paper Fortune-Teller back and forth and side to side while counting the chosen number. Make one movement for each count.

4. Now ask your friend to choose a number from the eight numbers showing inside the Paper Fortune-Teller. Again move the Paper Fortune-Teller while counting the chosen number.

5. Ask your friend to pick a number from the ones that can now be seen inside.

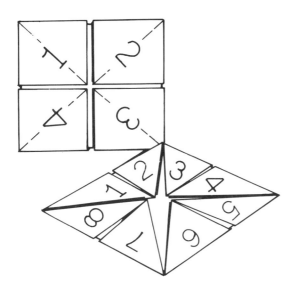

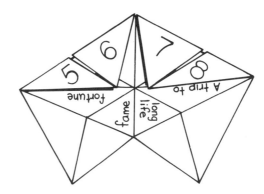

6. Lift the flap, and read the prediction written under that number.

SOME FORTUNATE PREDICTIONS

You can have fun writing your own predictions. Or try some of these traditional ones.

"You'll soon have money."

"You'll soon have a special reason to smile."

"One day you'll be famous."

"You'll find something you have lost."

"A wish will come true."

"You'll live a long time."

SMILE-MAKERS

Fill in the spaces for predictions with chores and favors your parents would enjoy—clean my room, mow the lawn, walk the dog. . . . Call *these* Paper Fortune-Tellers "Smile-Makers." You could give your mother or father a Smile-Maker for Mother's Day or Father's Day, and that will make your own future bright!

Roller Printing

This is a great way to make lots of prints quickly!

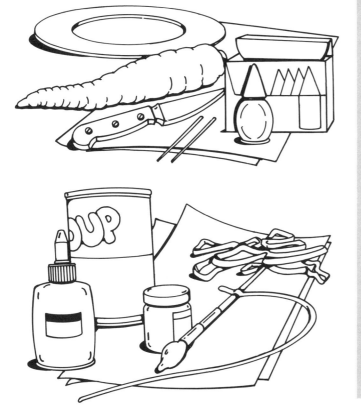

YOU'LL NEED

Stamp Pad (see p. 120)
paper for printing (plain note
    paper, white tissue paper,
    brown grocery bags, or
    construction paper)

Soup Can Roller

soup can
white liquid glue
several pieces of string, 12 to 18
    inches long *or* one or more
    large rubber bands
paint and brush

Carrot Roller

fat carrot
paring knife
two toothpicks
plate
food coloring *or* paint and brush

DIRECTIONS

Before beginning, cover the work surface with newspapers or plastic to protect it from stains.

With soup can rollers, designs can be larger and you can include several different designs on one can. These large roller printers are easy for small hands to use.

SOUP CAN ROLLER

1. Use an *unopened* soup can. You don't need to remove the label.

2. Cut small shapes from cardboard, and glue them around the can. *Or* dip string or rubber bands into glue and wind them around the can.

3. Allow the glue to dry.

4. Brush paint on shapes or on the string. You could also use a stamp pad.

5. Roll the soup can across the paper you chose.

Creating designs on carrot rollers takes a little patience since space is limited. But the designs will be delicate and produce natural, artistic results when you print.

CARROT ROLLER

1. Find a fat carrot and peel it.

2. Cut a 3-inch piece from the carrot. This piece should be fairly uniform in diameter.

3. With a paring knife, cut shapes and designs all around the carrot.

4. Place a toothpick at each end.

5. Put several drops of food coloring (p. 122) or natural dye (see p. 116) on a plate covered with plastic wrap and roll the carrot across the food coloring. *Or* you can brush carrot with paint, or use a stamp pad.

6. Roll the carrot across your paper.

ROLLER-PRINT DESIGNS

You can roll your printer across sheets of tissue paper or unfolded grocery bags to make your own original gift wrap.

Roll your printer across note paper or folded typing paper to make special note cards for yourself or for a friend.

Make roller-print pictures on construction paper and frame them.

And here's an idea! Use fabric paints (see p. 121) and roll designs across a T-shirt. After the fabric paint dries, you'll have a one-of-a-kind shirt.

What other ways can you use your new Roller Printer?

Magic Spectacles

Looking at the world through rosy red glasses can be wacky, wild fun. All kinds of funny and interesting surprises await you when you make these Magic Spectacles.

YOU'LL NEED

poster board, cardboard, or
    heavy paper
red cellophane or clean cellophane
    and red felt-tip marker
Popsicle® sticks
white liquid glue

DIRECTIONS

1. On poster board or heavy paper, draw two circles, each about 3 inches in diameter.

2. Inside each circle, draw another circle, leaving one-half inch all the way around.

3. Carefully cut out the smaller, inside circles.

4. From a piece of red cellophane, cut two 3-inch circles. If you cannot find any red cellophane, use clear cellophane or plastic wrap. Simply color the cellophane or wrap with a permanent red felt-tip marker.

5. Glue the cellophane circles to the poster-board circles.

6. Glue both circles to a Popsicle stick.

7. Wait until the glue dries, then look through the glasses to see a magical rosy world.

Magic Spectacles are wacky and wild, but

when you use them, you can also learn more about colors. *Primary colors* are red, blue, and yellow. *Secondary colors* are purple, green, and orange. Think about primary and secondary colors as you make and use your Magic Spectacles. Look at the *blue* sky through *red* glasses. What happens?

For extra fun and more color experiments, use blue or yellow cellophane in place of the red, or make several different pairs of Magic Spectacles!

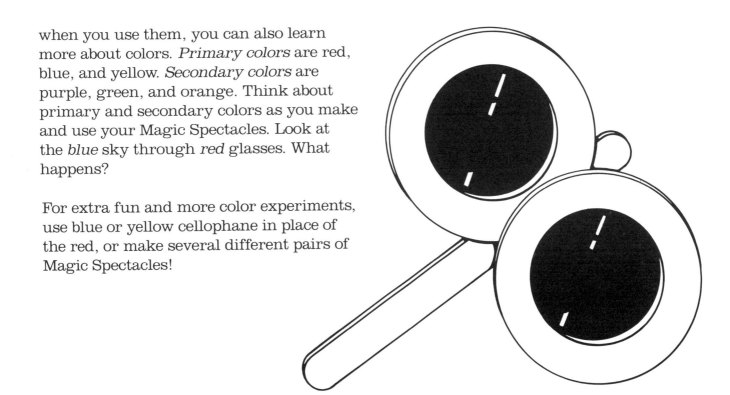

Flying Butterfly

These colorful paper butterflies make cute hanging decorations, but they can also be used for active play.

DIRECTIONS

1. Fold the construction paper in half.

2. Draw a butterfly wing pattern on the paper as shown.

3. Cut around the pattern lines, but do not cut the fold.

4. Unfold and decorate the wings with assorted scraps of construction paper, if desired.

5. Slide the butterfly's wings between the clothespin opening, and glue them to the clothespin.

6. Cut antennae from construction paper slightly longer than you wish them to be. Make a small fold at the bottom of each antennae, and glue them to the head of the clothespin.

7. Cut two pieces of thread, each about 30 inches long.

8. Tie one end of one piece of thread around the head of the clothespin, and knot, making knot side on top.

9. Tie other thread around the bottom of clothespin, about one-half inch from the bottom. Leave the knot side up.

10. Allowing butterfly to hang free, gather both threads together 12 to 18 inches from the base. Adjust threads so that the butterfly is balanced as it hangs, and make a knot in the two threads.

11. Gather threads at the top, and make a loop or another knot.

12. Using a thumbtack, tack the looped end of thread to the ceiling. Now your butterfly is ready to fly!

If you're careful, you can hold the top end of the thread and "fly" your butterfly indoors or outside.

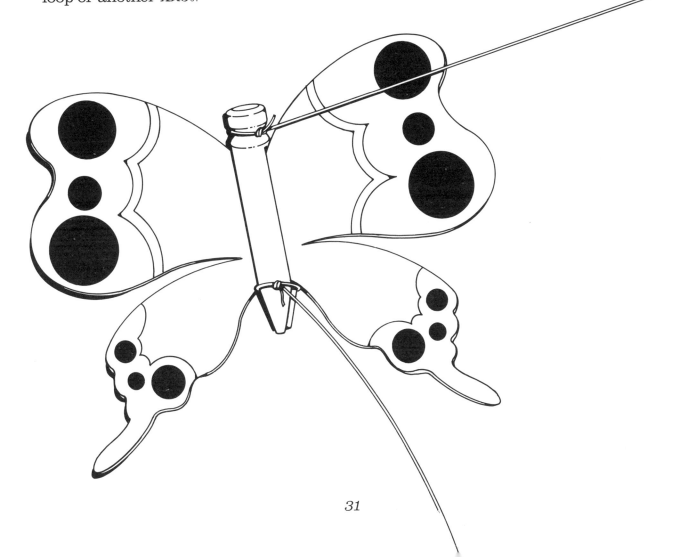

Shaving-Cream Sculptures

This is something everyone likes to get their hands into! If done in summer, both the picnic table and the sculptors can be quickly cleaned with a garden hose. That brings an extra sprinkle of fun!

YOU'LL NEED

large piece of plastic, old plastic tablecloth, or plastic place mat(s)
can of inexpensive shaving cream (enough for two children)
food coloring or water colors
smock or old shirt to protect clothing
spoons, Popsicle sticks, and other assorted items

DIRECTIONS

1. Cover work area with plastic.

2. Cover yourself with a smock.

3. Spray a large mound of shaving cream in front of you. Remember, this is *not* whipped cream, so don't eat it!

4. Use the spoon and other implements you've assembled to poke, scoop, and plop the shaving cream. How many different sculptures and designs can you create?

5. Drop one or two drops of food coloring on the mounds. Then make finger-paint designs. Experiment with color combinations, like yellow and blue, red and blue, or yellow and red. What happens if you mix the two colors together?

6. You can also make funny beards and moustaches on your own face, but be

careful not to get any in your eyes. It stings! Also, don't let the shaving cream stay on your face a long time. Wipe it off carefully with a damp cloth.

7. When you're finished sculpting, use paper towels to scoop the remaining shaving cream into a trash can. Rinse your hands in a sink or tub, then wipe off the plastic covering on the work area with a damp cloth.

Parents' Caution Don't allow children to pretend to shave with old razors, even with the blade removed. If the child finds a razor with the blade in place, that could be dangerous. Instead, substitute a spoon handle or Popsicle stick for "pretend" shaving.

Jack Frost Suncatchers

These delightful outdoor ornaments can be made year-round and kept in the freezer until Jack Frost settles in for the winter.

YOU'LL NEED

pie plate or cake pan
berries, flower blossoms, or snips
    from evergreen branches
long string or yarn
water

★ ★ ★ ★ ★ ★ ★

DIRECTIONS

1. Fill a pie plate or cake pan with water.

2. Carefully lay the string or yarn on top of the water around the edge of the pan. Let the ends of the yarn hang over the *outside* of the pan. (Leave enough yarn to tie the suncatcher to a tree when you've completed it.)

3. Arrange colorful berries, bits of pine branches, snips of flower blossoms, coils of apple peel, and other natural objects in the pan.

4. Place the pan in the freezer until the entire pan of water is frozen solid. (Make sure the pan sits flat.)

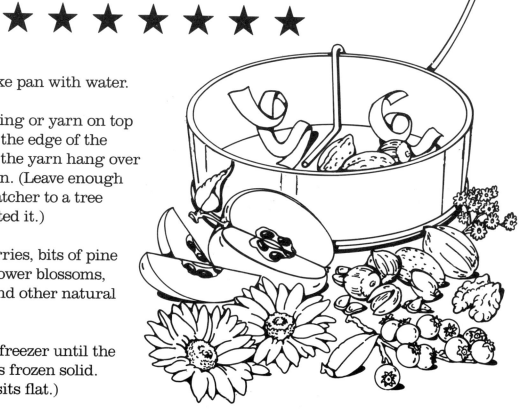

5. When Jack Frost arrives, and the temperature outside remains below 32 degrees Fahrenheit (0 degrees Centigrade), hang the suncatcher in a tree. Enjoy its shimmer as the winter wind plays upon the suncatcher. For warm seasons, store your suncatcher in a plastic bag, and keep it in a freezer until Jack Frost appears.

MORE IDEAS

Add a few drops of food coloring to the water before freezing it to get a "stained-glass" effect from the suncatcher.

Include birdseed with the berries and flower petals. When the temperature rises and the suncatcher begins to melt, birds will be able to peck through the ice for a snack.

Ghost-a-Notes

You can help your friends become amateur detectives and super-sleuths by sending them Ghost-a-Notes. And you don't even need to brew up any invisible ink for *this* mysterious writing!

YOU'LL NEED

2 sheets of paper
flat pan, larger than the paper
ballpoint pen

DIRECTIONS

1. Fill the pan with water.

2. Put one sheet of paper into the pan. When the paper is completely wet, *carefully* remove it, and place it on a flat surface.

3. Wet the second sheet of paper, and place it on top of the first sheet.

4. With the ball-point pen, write a message on the top sheet. Discard the top sheet after you've finished writing.

5. Allow the bottom sheet to dry completely. When it is dry, you won't be able to see the writing—*until* the paper is wet again!

IDEAS FOR GHOST-A-NOTES

- Send April Fools' Day cards to friends. Make a real, *visible* design on the outside of the card, and do your "ghost writing" inside.

- Use Ghost-a-Notes for birthday invitations. Use the ghost writing for the time, place, and name of the guest of honor.

- Write a mystery story for your friends to read, but use ghost writing for the important clues.

Remember to use *real* writing to explain how to get the message to appear: "To read the secret message, wet the paper!"

Hobbyhorse Puppet

Here's a chance to create one special pony friend or a corral full of characters for your own puppet show.

YOU'LL NEED

old sock *with* heel
old nylons, pantyhose, socks, or
    stuffing material
12-inch-long wooden dowel or
    sturdy twig
assorted rubber bands
white liquid glue
felt-tipped markers
yarn
4-inch square of cardboard

★ ★ ★ ★ ★ ★ ★ ★

DIRECTIONS

1. Stuff an old sock with stuffing material, or use old nylons or socks to stuff it. Fill the sock from toe to heel and just beyond. Leave 3 to 4 inches of the cuff unstuffed.

2. Insert a dowel or straight twig into the sock with the heel side up. Wrap a rubber band tightly around the outside of the cuff to hold the dowel in place. For added security, add some glue on the dowel inside the sock.

3. To make the horse's ears, grab up a little of the sock at the heel stitchings, then wrap each ear with small rubber bands.

4. Use felt-tip markers to make the horse's eyes, nose, and mouth.

5. Using about 7 yards of yarn, wind it

around the 4-inch cardboard square, letting both ends hang loose at the bottom.

6. While holding the yarn in place at the top of the cardboard, cut the yarn across the bottom.

7. Position the yarn on the horse's head to form the mane. Glue or stitch the yarn into place.

8. Cut a few strands of yarn, and position the strands on the horse's head so that it falls around the eyes. Glue or stitch the yarn strands into place.

After all the glue has dried, you're ready to have a galloping good time with your Hobbyhorse Puppet. Why not make several puppets with your friends and perform a "horsin' around" puppet show?

39

Floating Angels

This is a variation on a chain of paper dolls. After completing the floating experiment described below, even very young children can decorate these angels and use them as a tabletop Christmas display.

YOU'LL NEED

8½-by-11-inch paper
scissors
felt-tip markers, crayons, or
    colored pencils
white liquid glue
glitter

DIRECTIONS

1. Fold paper in half along the width, and cut along the fold into two 4¼-inch-by-11-inch strips. (Reserve one strip for another set of angels.)

2. Fold the strip in half as shown. Then fold the strip the same way two more times.

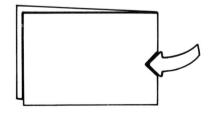

3. Copy the angel pattern onto the paper.

4. Cut all around the outline *except* at the ends of the wings and the skirt.

5. Open out the folded angels. If you wish, draw faces, hair, and other details on both the backs and fronts of the angels.

6. For fancy angels, spread a drop of white glue on the wings and halo. Then sprinkle them with glitter.

7. Stand the angels on a smooth surface, like a table, and blow gently. Your paper angels will "float" across the surface!

You can use the pattern at the bottom of the page for your own folding angel.

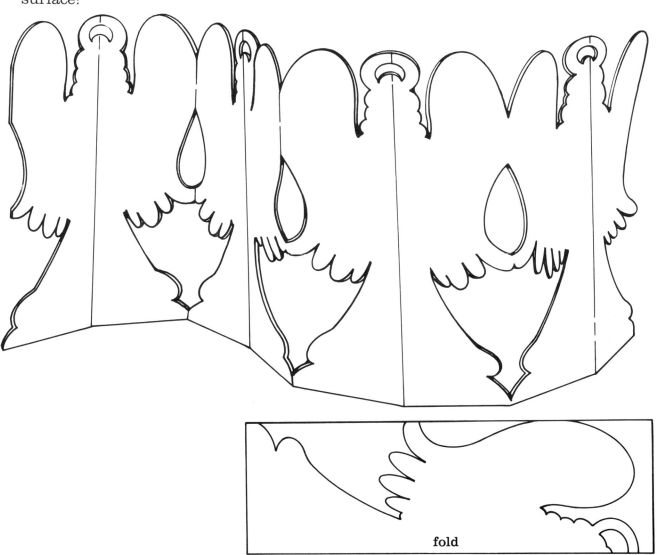

fold

Pinecone Flowers

YOU'LL NEED

pinecones
dried twigs or pipe cleaners
white liquid glue

DIRECTIONS

1. Cut the top off a pinecone, leaving the flower shape at the bottom.

   If you cannot find V-shaped twigs, substitute brown pipe cleaners. Add 2 inches to make the desired stem length. Wrap one pipe cleaner end around the pinecone's base.

2. To make the stem, use a dried twig with narrow branches that form a "V" at the top. Trim the twig to suit the stem length you desire. Trim the "V" branches so that the pinecone stem fits between them.

3. Put glue on the "V" branches, and fit them around the stem—or if there is no stem, the base of the pinecone.

4. Allow the glue to dry, and your pinecone flower is ready for a pretty vase.

Necklace-Face Folks

Necklace-face folks are sure to help curb boredom when you take them with you on long car trips.

YOU'LL NEED

8½-by-11-inch cardboard or poster board
old necklace chain, dark cord for pillows, *or* rolled shoelace
tape
colored markers

DIRECTIONS

1. Draw a side view (profile) of a person's head, but *do not* draw any of the features except an eye.

2. Make a hole in the poster board at the top of the head and another hole where the chin and neck will connect.

3. Pull one end of the chain or cord through the top hole, from the front of the picture to back, and tape one-half inch of chain on the back of the profile.

Repeat at the bottom hole with the other end of chain or cord.

4. Now gently push the chain around to create the forehead, nose, lips, and chin. You'll be able to give your Necklace-Face Folks very funny faces. And you can try out dozens of different profiles.

For additional fun, try drawing an animal's body and attaching the chain so that you can create unusual animal heads. Imagine a cat's body with the head of a horse or a horse's body with a pig's head!

Crayon Batik

Batik is a Javanese word that means "wax painting." This method of creating designs through the use of dyes and wax was first used by ancient Asian tribes in 3000 B.C. It was brought to Europe by Dutch traders in the 17th century. Ancient batik designs required many different materials and much time. With this crayon batik project, you can create batik-like designs quickly and easily.

DIRECTIONS

1. With the towel right side up, place your left hand on the towel's bottom, left side. Trace around your hand with a crayon.

2. On the towel's bottom, right side, a little higher than the tracing of your left hand, trace with a crayon around your right hand.

3. Above your handprints, neatly write the words "Helping Hands" with a crayon.

4. Now take a crayon and go back over all your crayon designs to make sure the colors and outlines are vivid.

5. Heat an iron to the cotton setting.

6. Place a thick layer of newspapers on the ironing board.

7. Place the towel *crayon side down* on the newspapers.

8. Press the towel with the hot iron for several minutes, moving the iron over the design area. Be careful not to scorch the fabric!

9. Remove the newspapers carefully, and replace them with another layer of newspapers. Press the towel again.

10. Let the towel cool completely, and remove the newspapers. Now you're ready to lend a helping hand in the kitchen.

You can use this method to create designs on T-shirts, too.

Launder crayon batik towels and T-shirts in cool water to retain their bright colors.

You can also create your own original designs on canvas tennis shoes. After you've drawn designs on your tennis shoes, tightly stuff the shoes with wadded newspapers. Then place newspapers on top of the crayon designs, and iron. Remove the iron from the surface of the newspapers frequently to prevent the paper from burning.

helping hands

Bookmark Corners

These handy bookmarks are so easy to make, you'll want to make several. They can even help you corner the spot for homework assignments in your schoolbooks.

YOU'LL NEED

3-by-3-inch square of felt or construction paper
needle and thread or glue

★ ★ ★ ★ ★ ★ ★

SEWING PROJECT

1. Fold the felt square in half diagonally, matching corners neatly.

2. Cut along the fold, making two identical triangles.

3. Pin the triangles together.

4. Sew along the two 3-inch edges with a running stitch or an overcast stitch. Use a thread color that contrasts with the color of the felt.

5. Knot the thread at the end of the second 3-inch edge, and remove the pins.

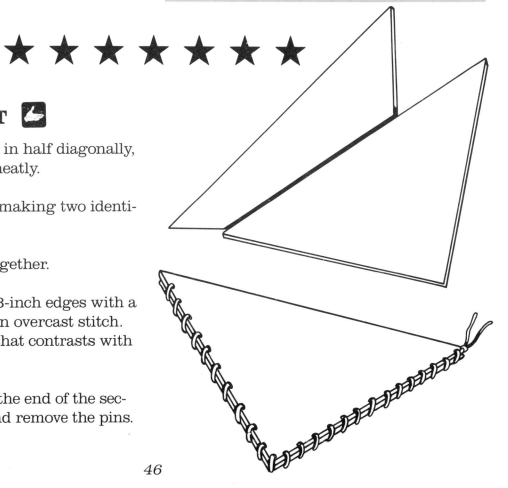

GLUING PROJECT

1. Using construction paper instead of felt, follow directions for the sewing project.

2. Glue the 3-inch edges together. Use the glue sparingly since you only want to glue the very outer edges of the bookmark.

3. Allow the glue to dry before using your bookmark.

Slip the open end of the bookmark over the top corner of the page you wish to mark.

If you want to decorate your bookmark corners, you can use glue and glitter or sew on sequins. But if you use glue, be sure that it's completely dry before placing the corner on a book page.

Block Printing

Block printing is an ancient art, practiced in Europe, Asia, and North and South America. Ancient Indian tribes used block prints to decorate their tools and clothing, and they sometimes created block-print designs on their bodies for special occasions. Indians used various objects from nature to create these printing blocks. You can create your own unique letter paper, note cards, or gift wrap with your own printing blocks made from natural objects or household things.

YOU'LL NEED

objects from nature—leaves, twigs banded together and cut evenly at one end, acorn caps, rocks with bumps and ridges
things from around the house— glass with a raised design, an old leather belt coiled and tied, celery and carrot slices, potatoes with carved-out designs
string, glue, wood block, or small cardboard box for *string printer*
watercolor paint, acrylic paint, or natural dye (see pp. 116–119)
Stamp Pad (see p. 120)
assorted paper

DIRECTIONS

1. If you use objects from nature, collect them. Be careful not to damage the plants and trees. Clean off any dirt or loose particles.

2. If you want to use items from around the house, collect and prepare them for printing. Coil and tie the belt. Make a clean cut at one end of the celery or carrot. Slice the rounded end from the

potato and carve a design. The *raised* portion of the potato design will print.

3. If you choose to use a string printer, add white glue to create a swirly, twisty design on the wood block or the bottom of the cardboard box. Lay the string carefully on the glue design, and allow it to dry completely.

4. To print, press the object to be printed onto the stamp pad. Make sure that all the design is covered with paint.

5. Firmly press the printer (potato, acorn, or what you choose to print) onto your paper, then lift the printer carefully.

6. Repeat steps 4 and 5 until you finish the design you want on your paper.

7. Allow the printed paper to dry thoroughly.

Eggshell Art

When you create a picture from many small pieces, the finished art is called a *mosaic*. Mosaic art dates back to ancient times. Ancient Egyptians made mosaic jewelry and decorated furniture from pieces of glass and stone. In India, marble mosaics adorn the outside of some buildings, and caskets and kitchen utensils were often decorated with materials such as wood, ivory, and shells. When you try Eggshell Art, you are actually creating a mosaic, and you can even use leftover shells from breakfast eggs or dyed Easter eggs.

DIRECTIONS

1. Break up eggshells into pieces no smaller than a dime.

2. If you are using the leftover peelings from hard-boiled Easter eggs, the coloring has already been done. If you are using white eggshells from breakfast, you'll need to color the shells.

Collect several small bowls or cups. Place ½ cup of water in each. Add ½ teaspoon of vinegar and several drops of food coloring in each bowl. Use one color for each bowl of water. Or, if you wish, dye the shells with natural dyes (see p. 116).

Place the broken shells in the bowls of food coloring, and allow them to stand for ½ hour.

Remove the shells and place them on paper towels to dry.

3. Spread white liquid glue on the cardboard or plywood, working in a small area at a time. Select pieces of eggshell and press them gently onto the glue. Arrange the shell pieces in a pattern, design, or picture.

4. Continue gluing eggshells to the cardboard or plywood until you cover the entire surface with shells. Allow the glue to dry.

5. Spray the finished design with a clear acrylic coating, and allow the paper to dry.

6. Glue a strong picture hanger to the back of the cardboard or plywood. Or use self-adhesive hangers. Your Eggshell Art is ready for hanging.

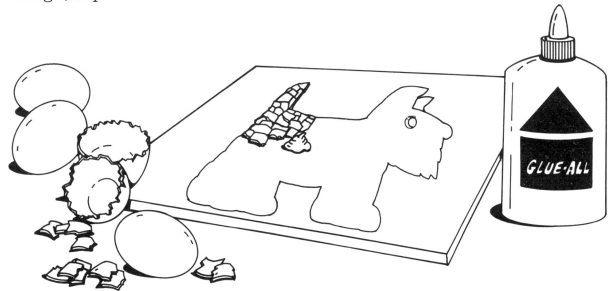

Lollipop Cookies

There are lots of creative possibilities for designing fancy cookies-on-a-stick. This is art you can eat—a project you can really sink your teeth into!

YOU'LL NEED

Sugar Cookies
    (see recipe on p. 108)
18 Popsicle sticks
1 or 2 baking sheets
rolling pin
Fast & Fabulous Frosting Glaze
    (see recipe on p. 112)
assorted sprinkles, colored sugar,
    or small candy pieces

DIRECTIONS

1. Mix the cookie dough. Wrap the dough in plastic, and refrigerate it at least 1 hour.

2. Sprinkle flour over the rolling surface. With a rolling pin, roll out the dough until it is about ¼-inch thick. Use a small juice glass to cut out circles of dough.

3. Place one of the dough circles on a baking sheet.

4. Place one Popsicle stick on top of the dough circle, about halfway up the middle.

5. Place another circle of dough on top of the first one on the cookie sheet. With your finger, press lightly all around the circle to blend the two pieces of dough together.

6. Continue to do the same thing with the rest of the cookie dough circles. Leave a 1-inch space between each lollipop cookie and its Popsicle stick.

7. Bake the cookies in a preheated oven at 375 degrees Fahrenheit for 10 to 12 minutes. Immediately remove the cookies from baking sheet, and let them cool slightly.

8. To decorate the cookies, make a batch of frosting glaze.

9. With a flat knife or spatula, spread a little frosting on top of a cookie. Quickly—before the frosting hardens—add sprinkles, colored sugar, or small pieces of candy.

10. After you frost all the cookies, there's just one thing left to do—EAT THEM!

You can make Halloween cookie pops. Simply color your frosting orange, and add candy corn for jack-o'-lantern faces. Or how about Valentine pops? Use heart-shaped cookie cutters and pink frosting. For Easter you could decorate egg-shaped cookies.

Dough for drop cookies can also be baked lollipop-style. See Chocolate Drop Pop recipe on p. 110.

Stained-Glass Butterflies

Louis Comfort Tiffany was an American artist who invented a method for making iridescent glass. He then fashioned art objects from this unique stained glass. When the objects were backlit by sunshine or light bulbs, the vibrant colors of the glass were stunning. Authentic Tiffany art objects are rare and very valuable today, but you can create a wonderful stained-glass effect when you make these paper butterflies.

DIRECTIONS

1. Place the two sheets of construction paper on top of each other. Fold them in half.

2. Draw a wing pattern on the folded construction paper as shown.

3. Cut out the wings, but *do not* cut along the fold.

4. With the construction paper still folded together, make another small fold along the top of the wing. Then cut a random-shaped hole in the small folded area.

5. Repeat this several times, making holes along the wing from top to bottom. Be careful so that the holes don't overlap.

6. Open up the wings, and set aside one of the wing patterns.

7. Cut a piece of colored cellophane (or tissue paper) to fit over one of the wings, without allowing the edge to overlap. Repeat for the other wing.

8. Glue cellophane to the wings.

9. Smear glue all around the wings, avoiding the hole areas.

10. Place the second wing pattern on top of the first, with the cellophane sandwiched in the middle. Line up the patterns carefully so that the holes match. Then press the two construction paper wings together, and allow the glue to dry.

11. Glue the middle section of the butterfly to one flat side of the clip clothespin. Let the butterfly dry.

12. After it dries, clip your butterfly where light will shine through. Window-shade pulls and curtain edges are nice spots for Stained-Glass Butterflies to rest. Or you could clip one to a lamp shade.

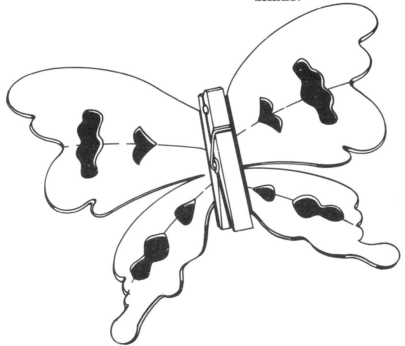

Sand-Castle Candles

YOU'LL NEED

shoe box
sand
candle wax, melted (old candle
    stubs)
candle wick
pencil or Popsicle stick

DIRECTIONS

1. Fill shoe box with damp sand.

2. Use your fist or a glass to make a hole in the center of the sand.

3. With your finger, poke four tunnels at least 1-inch deep at the bottom of the hole. Make sure that the tunnels connect to the hole and that they are spaced evenly around the hole. These tunnels will serve as the "feet" for your candle.

4. Wrap the candle wick around a pencil or Popsicle stick, and let one end fall to the bottom of the sand castle's hole. Position the pencil on top of the box so that the wick remains *straight*.

5. Melt the candle wax. (Use a double boiler, if you have one. However, an old pan directly on the burner will do.) Slowly pour the melted wax into the hole.

6. When the wax hardens, pull out the candle and brush off excess sand.

7. Set the candle on a heat-proof plate to protect the table or other surface it rests on.

Paper Snakes

Water is one of the main ingredients in making paper. When paper mills process magazine paper, much of the water is squeezed out to form the sheets. When the paper comes in contact with water again, it reacts in curious ways. You can watch the ways paper reacts to moisture, and also have fun when you make these paper snakes.

YOU'LL NEED

shiny magazine paper (*not* a
    magazine cover)
scissors
sponge

DIRECTIONS

1. Cut a wiggly-snake shape from shiny magazine paper. Cut a length of snake from the outside paper edge *toward the opposite edge.*

2. Saturate a sponge with water, and set it on a plate.

3. Place the snake, shiniest side up, on the sponge.

4. Watch carefully! As the paper absorbs moisture from the sponge, the snake will coil and dance.

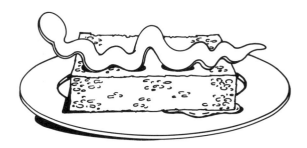

5. If you allow the paper snake to dry completely, you can use it over and over again.

Yarn Flowers

Flowers made from brightly colored yarn are pretty blossoms which can be enjoyed year-round.

YOU'LL NEED

yarn scraps in several colors
large marker with a ¾-inch diameter or larger base
8-inch green pipe cleaners (or color white pipe cleaners green)
5-inch green pipe cleaners

DIRECTIONS

1. Place an 8-inch yarn along the length of the marker. Hold the yarn firmly in place with your thumb and forefinger.

2. Use the same color of yarn to wrap the first yarn strand around the *diameter* of the marker twenty times, leaving 4 to 5 inches of yarn at each end.

3. Hold the marker so that all four yarn ends fall in the same direction.

4. Place the marker on the work surface, and tie a knot in the ends.

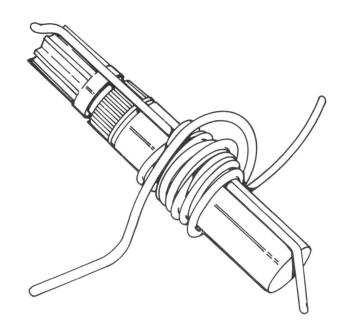

5. Hold the resulting yarn flower at the top, and carefully remove it from the marker.

6. Work an 8-inch pipe cleaner through the loop at the bottom of the flower. Bend the pipe cleaner, then twist it to form the flower's stem.

7. Separate the yarn loops to create the flower petals.

Repeat steps 1 to 7 to make more flowers in many colors.

Make leaves by bending 5-inch pipe cleaners into a "V", then twisting the open ends together around the stem. Shape the leaf however you wish.

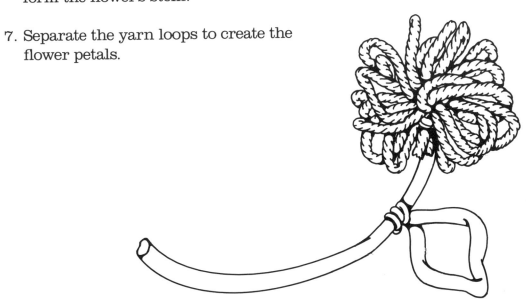

Summer Snowman

You don't need a blustery cold day or a thigh-high snowfall to make these any-weather snow sculptures.

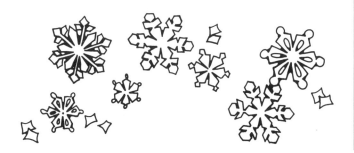

DIRECTIONS

1. Whip up a bowl of Soap Snow.

2. Wet your hands to keep snow from sticking to your fingers.

3. Pack the snow into three snowballs—large, medium, and small.

4. On the paper plate, stack the balls on top of each other, with the largest on the bottom up to the smallest.

5. Using assorted beads, buttons, and candies, give the snowman eyes, nose, and a mouth.

6. Tie a ribbon or fabric strip around the snowman's neck.

7. Use the paint or marker to color the spool black.

8. For the snowman's hat, cut a circle a little larger than the spool's diameter

out of the construction paper.

9. Glue the circle to one end of the spool.

10. Place the hat, with the paper side down, on your snowman's head.

For more ideas on what to do with Soap Snow, see the recipe file, p. 107.

Tooth-Fairy Pockets

These handy holders will keep baby teeth safe under a pillow or on a nightstand until the Tooth Fairy can collect them—and perhaps leave a shiny coin in their place!

YOU'LL NEED

3-by-8½-inch felt
scissors or pinking sheers
ruler
needle and thread
iron
permanent felt-tipped marker
glue and sequins or glitter

DIRECTIONS

1. With pinking sheers, pink the top 3-inch edge of the felt. Or use scissors to make a scalloped edge.

2. Measure 3½ inches up from the bottom, and fold it up toward the top of the felt.

3. Beginning at one of the top corners, sew the overlapping pieces of felt together. Use a running stitch or an overcast stitch. Sew around both sides and the bottom. If you like, use fabric glue instead of sewing two sides of felt.

4. Fold the top, scalloped edge over the sewn pocket. This will be the back of the pocket.

5. Press lightly with an iron.

6. On the front side of the pocket, carefully print your name with a permanent marker. Below that, print the word *tooth*.

7. If you wish, decorate your Tooth-Fairy Pocket with sequins and glitter. Then, when you lose a tooth, you'll have somewhere to keep it, or you can put it under your pillow for the Tooth Fairy.

Pinecone Creature Feeders

These pretty feeders hold and hide an edible treat for feathered and furry creatures alike. After you hang them outside, you'll soon see wildlife cavorting in your own backyard.

YOU'LL NEED

medium to large pinecones
18-inch piece of cord or ribbon
recipe of Crunchy Creature Stew
   (p. 113)

DIRECTIONS

1. Tie one end of the ribbon or cord around the upper part of a pinecone— about 1 to 2 inches from the top. Tightly tie and knot the cord.

2. Make a slip knot at the top end of cord.

3. Make some Crunchy Creature Stew. This recipe requires a stove or microwave.

4. Hold the pinecone at an angle over newspapers or a bowl, and drip globs of hot stew onto the pinecone "petals." As it cools, the stew will become thick.

5. When the pinecone is nicely filled,

hang your feeder from a tree branch or a hook near a window. That way, you'll be able to watch your visitors enjoy their treat.

Make more feeders to hang in your yard.

Try adding different ingredients to your Crunchy Stew recipe to see what kinds of critters you attract. (See recipe on p. 113.)

PROJECTS WITH STYLE

but they take a while

Mouse in a Cradle

YOU'LL NEED

can of white Play-Doh or home-
    made Flour Dough, Salt Dough,
    or Cornstarch Clay (see recipes
    on pp. 102, 104, and 106)
small scraps of fabric
whole walnuts, unshelled
heavy thread, yarn, or 1/16-inch
    ribbon
white liquid glue
cotton balls
fine-line black felt-tip marker

★ ★ ★ ★ ★ ★ ★

DIRECTIONS

1. Carefully crack and shell the walnuts, taking care not to break the halves. Each cleaned-out half shell will make one cradle.

2. Roll a little modeling dough into a ball the size of a large pea. This will be the mouse's head. Take half that amount for each ear. Roll the dough into two small balls; then flatten each. Carefully press the ears onto the head.

3. Attach the entire head to a piece of dough ½ to 1 inch long. Since you won't be able to see the body when the project is finished, you need not be fussy about the shape. Just make sure the mouse's body is not too long to fit into the cradle.

4. Place the mouse in a place to dry. This will take several days. If you want to speed up this part, put the mouse on a foil-lined cookie sheet, and bake it for 1 to 2 hours at 250 degrees Fahrenheit. Allow it to cool and dry for at least 24 hours.

5. Draw a face on the mouse's head with the marker—sleeping eyes, a nose, and whiskers.

6. Using half of the walnut shell, place a little cotton inside to make a "pillow" for your mouse. Glue the cotton to the shell.

7. Glue the mouse to the cotton.

8. Cut a small square of fabric, about 1½ inches, for the cradle blanket. Tuck the blanket around the sleeping mouse, up to his "chin." Glue it in place, using a few drops of glue on the mouse and the shell.

9. Cut two pieces of thread or narrow ribbon 8 inches long. Glue one ribbon lengthwise underneath the shell, allowing both cut ends to meet under the shell.

10. Repeat this with the second ribbon, gluing the second ribbon around the shell's width.

11. Gather the two ribbons together at the top of the shell so that the cradle hangs evenly. Glue the ribbons together at the top, or use a small piece of ribbon or thread to tie them together.

This small sleeping mouse makes a cute Christmas tree decoration or tie-on for wrapping gifts. The little fellow will also be quite comfortable rocking from a window-shade pull or from a decorative hook in your room.

Is there a special place in your house for a quiet little mouse?

Tin-Punch Pictures

Tinware has been used at least since the Bronze Age, since bronze is an alloy of copper and tin. Tinplate art was developed in Mexico in about 1650 when Spain restricted the availability of silver. And since tin was so inexpensive, it was commonly used by smiths and craftspeople in 18th and 19th century Europe and America as a substitute for silver and pewter.

You'll find it easy and inexpensive to use old tin-punch techniques to make lovely new pictures.

You can find tinplate at craft or hardware stores. And some old local newspapers still use it. You might be able to buy some from your hometown paper.

YOU'LL NEED

sheet of tinplate
scissors
hammer
nails
pattern for your design
cardboard, several sizes larger
    than your tinplate piece
masking tape
felt-tip marker
tracing paper
ruler
paper towels
window cleaner
picture frame

DIRECTIONS

1. Decide what size you want your picture to be. A good size to start with is 5 inches by 7 inches, since it easily fits into an inexpensive frame.

2. Choose your pattern. Find a picture

with a simple design. Preschool coloring books often have large, easy pictures which make great patterns. You can also find patterns in cross-stitch books and stencil-design books. Be sure the design fits inside the picture frame size you've chosen.

3. If the pattern you want to use is on a piece of paper you don't want to damage, such as a library book, copy the design on tracing paper. Keep your hand steady while you trace the pattern with a pencil. Or, if the design is on a loose sheet, you could make a photocopy. If it's OK to tear the pattern from a coloring book, tear it out carefully, and you're ready to go!

4. With a felt-tip marker, make *evenly spaced* dots around the outlines of the pattern. This will take patience, but it is important to space the dots just far enough apart so that each punch you make with a nail will be separate, but close to, the rest.

5. Cut the tinplate to the picture size you've chosen. Use your ruler, measure carefully, then cut with scissors. Be careful: The edges of cut tin can be very sharp!

6. If the tinplate came from a newspaper, clean the back (where the printing is) with a paper towel and alcohol or window cleaner.

7. Use masking tape to tape the tinplate—shiny side up—to the board.

8. Carefully center the design, then tape the pattern over the tinplate.

9. Place a nail on one black dot of your pattern, and tap it lightly with a hammer. You will not have to pound hard, since tinplate is thin and you only want a small hole for each pattern dot.

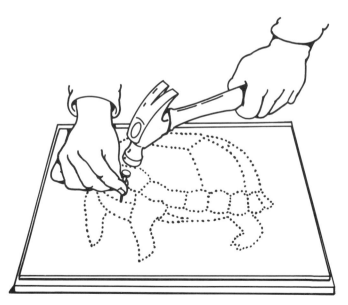

10. Continue punching around the dots of your design until you punch in all holes. Carefully lift one end of the pattern to make sure you haven't missed any dots. When you've finished, untape the pattern from the tin.

11. Remove the punched tin from the board, and carefully wipe it with a towel and window cleaner to remove any smudges.

Your tin-punch picture full of holes is ready for framing. Do not cover the picture with glass.

You could make a window ornament from the punched picture by gluing ribbon around the raw edges of the tin and tying a ribbon from the top. Sunlight will stream through the holes.

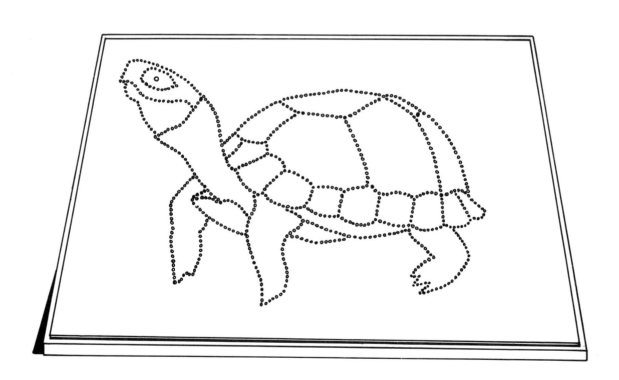

Dried Flowers

Before you begin to gather your favorite flowers for drying, here are some guidelines:

Do not pick *protected* species of flowers. Since only a small number of these species are left in the wild, leave them in their natural environment so that others can enjoy them. Also, many state or province laws prohibit picking flowers along roadsides, in public parks, and in nature preserves.

Avoid picking flowers without the permission of the property owner. Most gardeners are happy to share a few of their flowers, but don't be greedy. Only take a few.

Handle flowers that you want to dry with care. Use a sharp knife or scissors to cut the flower several inches down the stem. Don't pull the flowers from the ground since this can damage their root system.

Keep all flowers you collect in water until you can process them. This will keep the blossoms fresh.

It's best to process the flowers as soon as you can after picking, to help preserve their natural colors.

YOU'LL NEED

flowers picked on a dry, sunny day—remove all but 1 inch of the stem
24-ounce (670-g) box of yellow cornmeal or 3 cups (720 ml) of sand
1 cup (240 ml) of *uniodized* salt (iodized salt is OK, but flower colors will fade slightly)
shoe box with lid
sheets of waxed paper or paper towels
watercolor brush
wire stems
acrylic spray or hair spray (optional)

CORNMEAL AGENT

1. Collect flowers that are in full bloom. Only roses should be picked *before* they are in full bloom, since they continue to open during the drying process.

2. Strip all leaves—foliage—from the flower's stem, except one or two leaves near the blossom. If you prefer to have no leaves, that's fine.

3. Mix the cornmeal and the salt thoroughly. This is your *agent*.

4. Line the shoe box with waxed paper or paper towels.

5. Cover the bottom of the container with ½ inch of the agent—the cornmeal and salt mixture.

6. Place the flowers on top of the agent; leave at least 1 inch between blossoms.

Place larger flowers facedown and smaller ones faceup.

7. Use a teaspoon to add small amounts of the agent to the flower. Sprinkle the agent in and around the petals so that it covers the entire flower. Work on one flower at a time.

8. Dry just a single layer of flowers in one container.

9. Cover the container with the lid and allow the flowers to dry for 4 to 6 days. The larger the flower, the longer it will take to dry. Do not overdry. This will cause the petals to be brittle and break easily.

10. Check to see if the flowers are dry by gently pushing your finger through the agent; the petals should feel like thin paper. When the flowers are dry, carefully shake the box over a bowl or cookie sheet to remove the agent. Save the cornmeal-salt agent since you can use it again.

11. Gently push the agent away from the blossoms with your fingers. If any cornmeal-salt sticks to the flower, gently brush it off the petals with a small watercolor paintbrush.

12. Insert a wire stem into the piece of stem that you left on the flower. Be careful not to push the wire through the top of the blossom.

If you want to add a little shine to your flower, spray it lightly with acrylic spray or hair spray.

Make a bouquet of dried flowers, and place it in a vase to enjoy long after summer flowers have disappeared from gardens.

SAND AGENT

You can substitute sand for the cornmeal, since sand and salt also make an effective agent for preserving dried flowers. Simply use 3 cups (720 ml) of sand to 1 cup (240 ml) of salt.

Rhythm Sticks

Long ago, Native Americans made rhythmic music by rubbing two specially crafted sticks together. These rhythm sticks were called *guayos*. You can make your own rhythm sticks, similar to those made by Indians. Since you'll be using a sharp carving knife, this project should be done with an adult.

YOU'LL NEED

dowel or tree branch, 18 inches long
    and 1 to 2 inches in diameter
dowel or sturdy twig, 12 to 14 inches
    long and ½ inch in diameter
sandpaper
large, dried gourd (optional)
sharp knife

DIRECTIONS

1. Decide which side of the large dowel or branch you want to be the rhythm stick's top. If you are using a tree branch, remove the bark and any twig sections.

2. Cut notches along the rhythm stick's top, spacing these notches ¼ inch apart. Leave a 4-inch section unnotched at the end of the stick since it will be the handle.

3. If you use a twig for the top rubbing stick, peel off any bark, and sand the twig until it is smooth. If you use a dowel for the rubbing stick, you're ready to make music.

To play the Rhythm Sticks, rub the smooth, narrower stick across the notches in the wider stick. Turn on your radio or audiocassette player, and begin to create various rhythms to accompany the music.

To make the sound from your rhythm stick

louder, place the stick on a large, dried gourd; then rub the smooth stick across the notches. The hollow gourd will amplify the sound and make it easier to hear your music.

You can personalize your guayos by drawing designs on them with permanent-ink markers. Or, if you know someone with wood-burning tools, perhaps he or she would be willing to engrave your name or a design on the rhythm sticks for you.

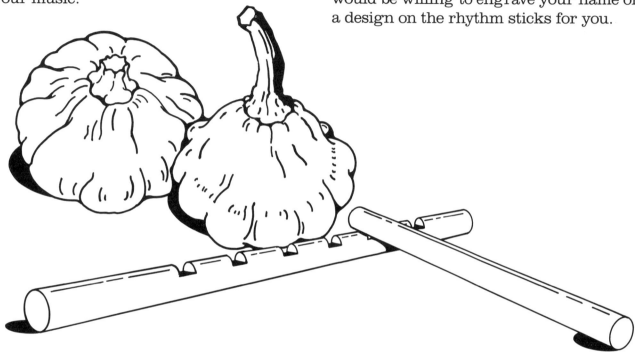

Spatter-Dyed Toy Bag

This can be a messy project. So, work outdoors, in the basement, or in the bathroom, where spills will be less of a problem. Wear rubber gloves, if you have them, and old clothes.

YOU'LL NEED

white pillowcase
food coloring
spray bottle filled with water
2 large plastic bags or sheets
newspapers
cord or ribbon 36 to 40 inches long
scissors or hole-punch

DIRECTIONS

1. Spread newspapers on your work surface.

2. Spread plastic on top of the newspaper.

3. Lay a *dry* pillowcase on top of the plastic. Place a piece of plastic *inside* the pillowcase, and smooth the pillowcase so that it lies flat.

4. With a food coloring bottle, sprinkle, splash, and dot color randomly on the pillowcase.

5. Repeat step 4 with all three remaining colors.

6. Using a spray bottle, wet the pillowcase with water. As the pillowcase gets wet, the colors will begin to merge and blend. Avoid drenching the pillowcase with water, but make sure the entire surface is damp.

7. Carefully turn over the pillowcase, and repeat steps 1 to 6 on the other side.

8. Pin the pillowcase at its corners to a

hanger, and hang it up to dry. Since the pillowcase will drip as it dries, be sure to protect the area under the pillowcase with newspapers or plastic.

9. When the pillowcase is *completely dry*, use a pencil or black marker to mark along the pillowcase's entire hem. Space dots 2 inches apart and 2 inches away from the pillowcase's open end.

10. With sharp scissors or a hole-punch, poke holes all the way through the pillowcase at each marked dot. You could sew buttonholes around each hole, but it isn't necessary.

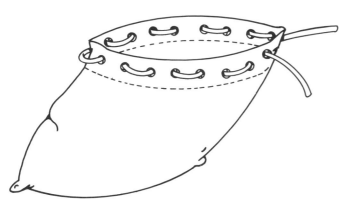

11. Work narrow cord or ribbon through the holes, beginning with one of the middle front holes and ending with the other middle front hole.

12. Make a big knot in each end of the cord; this will keep the cord from slipping back through the holes. To close your toy bag, pull both ends of the cord at the same time.

If you have an old white T-shirt that's stained, you can use this spatter-dyeing method. That way, stains will seem to disappear and you'll be able to wear your wild and wacky shirt.

After the toy bag or shirt dries, it's a good idea to set the colors. Soak the bag or shirt for ½ hour in a solution of ½ cup of vinegar, ½ cup of water, and 3 tablespoons of salt. Then allow the bag or shirt to dry again.

Wait at least 48 hours after dyed pillowcases or T-shirts have completely dried before you wash them. Wash them separately.

To create a wild, WOW! outfit, splatter-paint a pair of painter's white overalls with fabric paint and wear them with one of your "designed-it-myself" T-shirts.

The best way to "paint" a T-shirt, of course, is with fabric paints made specially for this purpose. Also, they don't come off in the wash.

HURRY-UP METHOD

Some craftspeople are more focused on the finished results of a project than on the creative process itself. For these folks (and those who want a quicker, less messy method), ready-to-use fabric paints (see p. 121) will be more reliable in producing consistent results.

Simply splatter the fabric paints onto the pillowcase (as outlined in the previous directions), then roll up or fold the pillowcase to blend and merge the colors. You'll greatly reduce processing and drying time with this method.

78

Clay Dolls

YOU'LL NEED

Sculpting
Cornstarch Clay (see recipe on
  p. 106)
toothpicks
assorted carpenter nails
sharp pencil
aluminum foil
shortening
baking sheet

Painting
acrylic paints
cotton balls, yarn, or furry fabric
clear acrylic spray

Creating the Doll's Body
white liquid glue
large sheets of plain paper
cotton fabric, in a solid color
quilt stuffing or old nylons
needle and thread (sewing machine)
safety pins
heavy hand-sewing needle
heavy thread (buttonhole twist or
  carpet thread)

Dressing the Doll
plain paper
assorted clothing fabric
needle and thread (sewing machine)

This four-part project should not be rushed. So, gather materials and patience, and you'll create a one-of-a-kind doll. Be sure to read *all* directions before you begin. You can even celebrate important people from history, if you wish. Sew a costume for a pirate, Viking, explorer, American Indian, sharpshooter, or ancient queen.

SCULPTING

1. Make Cornstarch Clay according to the recipe on p. 106.

2. Using the clay, sculpt the head and shoulders as one unit. (See the diagram below). For support, push a

toothpick or thin nail through the center of the head to the shoulder section. Cover the hole made by the nail at the top of the head with clay.

3. Create the doll's face—eyes, nose, mouth, and ears—by carving them with a toothpick, sharp pencil, or fingernail. Carefully work the clay to form cheeks, chin, forehead, and eyebrows, if you want lots of definition.

4. Hollow out the shoulder section, and poke holes into the front and back of the shoulders with a carpenter's nail (see illustration). Since these holes will be used to attach the body to your doll, be sure they will allow a needle and thread to pass through.

5. Mold feet and hands, making them extra long so that you can glue on the arm and leg sections later. If necessary, use toothpicks for extra support.

6. Cover a baking sheet with lightly greased foil.

7. Crumple a small piece of foil to fill the shoulder cavity and support the head section. If possible, place the torso upright on the baking sheet. Otherwise, lay it down faceup.

8. Also place the doll's feet and hands on the baking sheet.

9. Bake them at 200 degrees Fahrenheit for 2 to 3 hours. Let all doll parts cool and dry completely—at least 24 hours.

PAINTING

1. Use acrylic paints to paint the doll's face, eyes, mouth, hands, and feet or shoes. Allow the paint to dry.

2. To preserve your painted doll, spray all the clay parts with clear acrylic spray. Apply two light coats, and allow each coat to dry completely.

3. Use cotton balls, yarn, or snipped pile from a furry fabric to glue hair, eyebrows, or even a beard to your doll.

CREATING THE CLOTH BODY

1. Draw a pattern on plain paper for your doll's body. Make the pattern outline about one inch larger all the way around than you want the finished body. The pattern can be the same for both boy and girl dolls.

2. Cut two identical pattern pieces out of cotton fabric.

3. With right sides together, stitch around the outline of the fabric pieces (see dotted lines below). Leave arm, leg, and shoulder openings unstitched. Turn the finished garment right side out.

4. Pin the arm and leg openings closed with safety pins, and stuff body until it becomes quite firm.

5. Remove pins from the openings, and gently push the clay leg and arm pieces into place. Glue the doll's arms and legs to the fabric, and allow them to dry.

6. Glue the shoulder and head unit to the fabric in the same way.

7. Use strong thread—like buttonhole twist or carpet thread—and a needle to attach the fabric through the holes in shoulder piece.

DRESSING THE DOLL

1. Using the paper pattern for a guide, make more patterns for shirts, pants, or a dress. Remember that the clothes must fit over the doll's stuffed body; so, your clothing patterns must be at least 1½ inches larger than the original pattern for the doll's body.

2. Cut patterns from any fabric you like, and sew the clothing by hand or by machine. Felt and polyester fabrics are easy to work with since their raw edges do not fray.

3. After you help the doll into his or her outfit, you are done. Remember that your finished doll will be fragile; so, handle it with care.

You may be able to find ready-made doll clothes that fit your doll. Also, some fabrics can be glued together, eliminating the need for sewing.

To safely display your doll, you could use a doll stand.

HISTORICAL DOLLS

For an extra-credit school project or simply for the fun of it, you can make historical dolls. This is an opportunity to experiment with making beards, unusual hairdos, and replicas of unique historical clothing and accessories. Before plunging into this project, though, you'll want to read about the specific historical figure you wish to represent so that the doll will be as authentic as possible. Here are some possibilities:

Abraham Lincoln He has a beard and a fun-to-make hat!

Annie Oakley Go ahead; test your creativity. Can you make a miniature gun and holster for her?

Benjamin Franklin Fine wire or an old egg-dipper can be crafted into spectacles for wise old Ben.

Elizabeth I of England Complete with 16th century royal regalia?

Amelia Earhart Aviator extraordinary. What did she wear on long-distance flights?

Kit Carson His western outfit and bushy moustache are challenging, but fun.

What other historical dolls can you think of? It might be fun to make dolls of *ancients*—Hannibal, Al-Khansā, Ptolemy, Cleopatra, Lao-tzu, Viking Eric the Red; *Middle Ages and Renaissance*—Christine de Pisan, Joan of Arc, Galileo Galilei, Johannes Gutenberg, Henry VIII of England, Henry Hudson; *17th and 18th century*—pirate Sir Henry Morgan, Mary Wollstonecraft, Sacajawea, Betsy Ross; *19th and 20th century*—Harriet Tubman, Sojourner Truth, Dame Nellie Melba, Chief Red Cloud, Mahatma Gandhi, Mary Pickford, or Clara Barton.

Or you could make dolls of one or more *fictional characters* from books of the Brontë sisters (Anne, Emily, and Charlotte), Beatrix Potter, Arthur Conan Doyle, Mark Twain, Miguel Cervantes de Saavedra, or your favorite author.

Dandy Rock Candy

It's extremely easy to make candy on a string. But you'll need lots of patience. It sometimes takes two weeks for big, chunky crystals to form.

Whenever a solid develops from a liquid, the result is a *crystal*. *Diamonds* are crystals which are formed far below the earth's surface. *Table salt* contains many perfect crystals, although you cannot often see them without the aid of a microscope. And frozen water—*ice*—is a crystal, too. When you make rock candy, you are actually performing a scientific experiment. In the end, you have the added bonus of a sweet treat to eat!

Although it's quite simple to make candy crystals, you do need to wait a little. Since temperature variables will affect the growth of crystals, it could take as long as a couple of weeks to make rock candy, and the size of the final crystals can range from small, pearl-size candy to walnut-size whoppers.

As with all scientific experiments, you will learn from trial and error, so keep trying until you are happy with the results.

YOU'LL NEED

1 cup (240 ml) of water
4 cups (1 kg) of sugar
blue food coloring
pint-sized (480 ml) canning jar
quart-size (1 l) cooking pot or bowl
string
pencil

DIRECTIONS

Use a conventional stove or a microwave to begin to form your candy crystals.

1. If you use the *stove*, pour 1 cup of water into a quart-size pot. Add 2 cups of sugar, and stir over medium heat until the sugar dissolves completely. Do *not* boil. Gradually add the remaining 2 cups of sugar and 2 drops of the blue food coloring. Continue to stir until all the sugar is completely dissolved. Be careful—you can be badly burned by melted sugar.

   If you use a microwave instead of a stove, place 1 cup of water in a microwavable 1-quart bowl. Stir in 2 cups of sugar and microwave for five minutes on HIGH. Remove and stir. Be very careful. The bowl and the sugar water will be very hot! Repeat the microwave process until all the sugar is completely dissolved. Stir in the remaining 2 cups of sugar and 2 drops of blue food coloring. Continue to microwave at 3- to 5-minute intervals until all sugar is dissolved.

2. Carefully pour the sugar water into a clean glass jar.

3. Cut the string into three pieces so that each piece is about 12 inches long.

4. Tie each string around the pencil so that all six ends can hang down into the sugar water when the pencil is placed across the rim of the jar. Do *not* let the strings rest on the bottom of the jar.

5. Now comes the hard part, waiting. Set the jar someplace where it will not be disturbed. About every other day, use a spoon or knife to *gently* break up the crystals which cover the top of the sugar water. But be careful not to stir the water or lift the strings. Just wait. And wait.

6. In about 1 to 2 weeks, you will have some nice, big sugar crystals, and some yummy rock candy!

Tin-Punch Lantern

In colonial days, many houses were lit by candles placed in tinplate *lanthorns*, a word that dates from the 16th century and means "lanterns." Punched holes admit oxygen and allow light to shine through. You can make your own simple version of a colonial lanthorn to use as a candle holder.

DIRECTIONS

1. Remove the lid and the label from a tin can.

2. Fill the can with water, and freeze it until the water becomes solid ice.

3. Choose your pattern. (See directions for making tin-punch designs on pp. 68–69.) Make a design all the way around the can, or use just one side.

4. Lay the can containing frozen water on its side atop newspapers or a towel.

5. Tape the pattern to the can. Leave a ½ inch margin around the bottom of the can. This will prevent melted wax from leaking through the punched holes.

6. Pound a nail into each dot of your pattern on the can.

7. When you finish punching in the design, remove the paper pattern and the ice. Put a candle inside the can.

8. Place this candle holder on a heat-proof surface, since the heat from the candle will make the can quite hot.

Enjoy the lovely light designs that flicker from your lanthorn.

Miniature Maracas

It is thought that the first musical instruments were percussion instruments. Sound was produced when one object hit another object. Maracas are percussion instruments that originated in Brazil. Most maracas are made of dried gourds or round rattles with pebbles in them. You can make small maracas out of walnut shells.

　　You can use them to accompany spicy Latin salsa or Latin jazz beats. The music is lots of fun to dance to.

YOU'LL NEED

walnuts
white liquid glue
Popsicle sticks
small beads, buttons, or seeds
paint or nail polish
file or sandpaper
rubber band

DIRECTIONS

1. Carefully open a walnut so that you have two uncracked halves.

2. Remove everything inside the shells. Save the nutmeats for a quick snack.

3. Sand or file the shell's flat bottom end so that you can insert the Popsicle stick and fit the shell halves together.

4. Place one or a few tiny buttons, dried apple seeds, cherry pits, or small beads inside one half-shell. Avoid crowding the shell so that your maraca will be able to make noise.

5. Drop a little glue on the edge of one shell half.

6. Glue one end of the Popsicle stick.

7. Put both halves of shell together, with the Popsicle stick in between.

8. Wind a rubber band around the shell to hold both halves tightly together until the glue dries. This will take several hours.

9. If you wish, decorate your maraca with acrylic paints, or cover it with a clear varnish or nail polish.

Create your own percussion by gently shaking your maraca.

Invite some friends to help you create a percussion band. With several walnut maraca instruments and one or more Rhythm Sticks (p. 74), you'll soon be rockin' with the rhythm. With a few Hullabaloo Kazoos (p. 20), you can add strange and wonderful wind-instrument melodies to your performances. Compose your own new spicy Latin music, or accompany your favorite records.

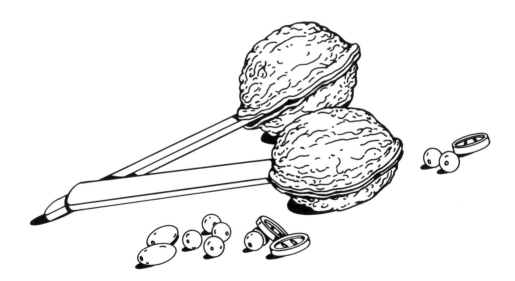

Burlap Baskets

Baskets made from burlap are lovely alone, but they can also become containers for your dried flower or yarn flower creations. And they are wonderful when filled with home-made potpourri.

DIRECTIONS

1. Cut the burlap into a circle about 11 inches in diameter.

2. Place the burlap circle in a large mixing bowl, and squeeze white liquid glue onto the burlap.

3. Thoroughly saturate the burlap with the glue, working the glue into the burlap with your hands. This is gooey work! Wash your hands after the burlap is completely soaked with glue.

4. Wrap plastic wrap around the outside of the small bowl, glass, or muffin dish. Stuff excess plastic wrap inside the bowl or glass.

5. Now, the work gets messy again. Take the gluey, mushy burlap and place it on a flat surface covered with plastic wrap. Place the bowl in the center of the circle of burlap.

6. Mold the burlap around the bowl. Make a ruffled edge at the top. Use scissors to make the edge even, if necessary. Wash the scissors after you use them or they'll be sticky ever after.

7. Set the basket on a plastic-covered surface to dry.

8. When the burlap is thoroughly dry, remove the small bowl. Wash the bowl in hot water to remove any traces of glue.

9. Tear the plastic wrap out of the burlap basket's inside.

You could use this basket for party nut cups. You could also make flower arrangements with dried flowers and hold them together with florists' clay. If you want to make the basket a little water-resistant, you can put plastic inside.

Baked Napkin Rings

Napkin rings made from ready-to-use biscuit dough add a touch of class to any table setting. For special occasions, tie a narrow ribbon into a bow around the top of the napkin ring.

YOU'LL NEED

tube of refrigerator biscuits
aluminum foil
cookie sheet
clear acrylic spray
heavy pot (used as weight)

DIRECTIONS

1. Crumple a large piece of aluminum foil into a tube, about 8 to 10 inches long and 1½ inches in diameter.

2. Line the cookie sheet with foil.

3. Cut one unbaked biscuit into three equal pieces.

4. Roll each piece of dough into a thin rope.

5. Pinch one end of each rope together. Press the pinched ends onto your work area and weight them down with a heavy skillet or pot. Or work with a partner, and take turns holding the pinched-together ropes in place.

6. Braid the dough ropes, but leave a small end of each rope unbraided.

7. Carefully wrap the braid loosely around the foil tube to form a circle. Pinch the ends together.

8. Place the tube on a cookie sheet with the pinched ends of braid on the bottom.

9. Make several braided rings, and place

each one on the foil tube, leaving 2 inches between each ring.

10. Bake at 250 degrees Fahrenheit (121 degrees Centigrade) for one hour.

11. Carefully remove the foil, and allow the dough rings to cool.

12. Place the cooled rings in a dry place for at least 2 days.

13. Cover the work area with newspapers, and spray the bottom and inside of the dough rings with acrylic spray. Allow the rings to dry completely, then spray the top of the rings. Allow the tops to dry.

A set of four or six napkin rings makes a very nice gift.

How about making tiny braided rings to be used with scarves, neckerchiefs, and sashes?

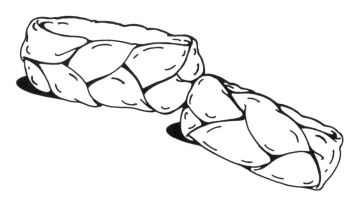

Apple-Head Doll

Apple carving is an old art, but the results are always surprising. Since the fruit shrinks as it dries, the carvings on the face change, and the doll appears to "age" before your very eyes.

YOU'LL NEED

medium or large green apple
lemon juice
paring knife
pencil
2 whole cloves
liquid dish detergent bottle and cap
sand or dried rice
cotton or yarn
2 pieces of 18-by-18-inch fabric
white liquid glue

DIRECTIONS

Here's how you prepare the head of the Apple-Head Doll and carve his or her face.

1. Pare the apple. Do this very carefully to remove the skin but keep the surface as smooth as possible.

2. Remove a small amount of core from the bottom.

3. To carve the face, use a small paring knife. Make deep cuts for eyes. For the nose, cut wedges on each side for cheeks so that the nose sticks out a bit. Make a slit for the mouth. If you want more detail, you can also sculpt the cheeks and chin by carving away small bits of apple from those areas. But remember, just make *shallow* cuts.

4. Use your fingernail or a straight pin to

scrape wrinkles into the forehead, cheek, and chin areas.

5. Soak the apple in lemon juice for 15 minutes.

6. Lightly dry the apple with a paper towel, and insert a pencil at the bottom of the apple, where you removed the core.

7. To dry your apple head, put a pencil into a jar or bottle, making sure that the apple does not touch *anything* as it dries. If anything touches the apple while it dries, that could cause the apple to spoil.

8. Allow 3 to 4 weeks for your apple head to dry.

9. On the *second day* of the drying time, poke whole cloves into the eye holes.

10. On the *sixth day* of the drying time, remove the pencil from the apple head, and place the head on the pull-up cap of a plastic dish-detergent bottle.

11. After the drying time is complete, glue the head to the bottle cap, if necessary.

12. Fill the detergent bottle with sand or dried rice to prevent the doll from tipping over. Screw the cap with the apple head onto bottle.

13. For the Apple-Head Doll's dress, drape fabric around the bottle, with the fabric's raw edges in back. Cut the fabric to fit the bottle, and allow for fullness at the shirttail or the skirt's bottom. Glue the fabric together, then glue it to the back of the bottle.

14. Glue cotton balls or yarn to the doll's head for hair. Allow the glue to dry.

15. Fold the cape fabric in half diagonally, then cut it to the size you want. Be sure to make it long enough to tie.

16. Position the cape on the doll's head, and tie it in front, under the chin. Make sure the tied knot does not leave any of the bottle exposed. Adjust the fabric, and use glue, if necessary.

Each Apple-Head Doll you make will seem to have a personality all its own, depending on the facial features you create and the way the apple dries. You can make an outfit for each doll by experimenting with different fabrics. You could use ruffles to cover the neck instead of a cape.

Wishing Pin

Instead of breaking the wishbone from a roasted chicken or turkey to make a wish come true, leave the wishbone whole and make a good-luck pin that you can keep handy for months. May all of your wishes come true!

DIRECTIONS

1. Thoroughly wash the wishbone from a turkey or chicken, and allow it to dry for several days.

2. Use acrylic paint or nail polish to paint one side of the wishbone. Allow the paint to dry. Paint the other side.

3. Tie a ribbon around the head of a safety pin, and knot it securely. Add a little glue to the back of the knot.

4. With the glue-side of the knot against the wishbone's neck, tie a ribbon around the other side of the neck. Add a spot of glue between the ribbon and wishbone. Knot the ribbon tightly. Finish with a pretty bow.

Mosaic Medallions

Shimmery! Sparkly! These mosaic medallions make lovely jewelry or wall plaques, and you can create them in minutes.

YOU'LL NEED

Salt Dough (see recipe on p. 104)
glasses in assorted sizes
objects for creating designs—fork,
    straw, cookie stamps, things
    with raised or depressed designs
aluminum foil
plastic wrap or waxed paper
rolling pin
cookie sheet
ribbon or string
beads, glitter, or other decoration

DIRECTIONS

1. Make Salt Dough according to the recipe.

2. Place the dough on a piece of aluminum foil.

3. Place plastic wrap or waxed paper on top of the dough, and roll it out to the desired thickness. About ½ inch works well for small creations, like necklaces. Remove the plastic wrap.

4. Choose a drinking glass the size you want to make your circle. Turn it upside down on the dough and press down firmly to cut the dough into a circle. Carefully lift the glass. Make several circles in various sizes.

5. Using the straw, press a hole near the top of the round medallion. Make sure that you remove all the dough from the hole.

6. Use forks and other objects, such as cookie stamps, to create patterns and designs on the medallion. For a lacy look, cut shapes completely through the dough. For an engraved look, do not press your designs deeply into the dough.

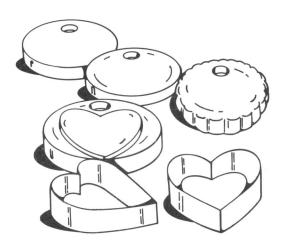

7. When you finish designing the medallions, carefully lift the foil and the medallions onto the cookie sheet. Wrap any leftover dough in plastic wrap. The Salt Dough will not stay moist for more than a few days.

8. Bake the medallions for several hours at 200 degrees Fahrenheit until they are completely dry. The dough will also dry at room temperature in 3 to 5 days.

9. Allow the salt dough medallions to cool. Then remove the foil from the back of the baked medallions. Beads, glitter, and other decorations may be glued into place after baking, if you wish.

10. Pull ribbon or string through the top hole, and knot it. You can wear your medallion anywhere or use it as a wall plaque.

MORE IDEAS

Make Christmas tree decorations by rolling out the Salt Dough and cutting shapes from holiday cookie cutters.

Sprinkle small amounts of glitter randomly on the unbaked objects, then press them lightly so that the glitter will stick to the dough as it bakes.

Make small, freestanding figurines. Perhaps you can craft a miniature crèche (manger scene) to display at Christmastime or sparkly little angels to adorn a holiday buffet table.

RECIPE FILE

doughs, paints, inks & stinks

Flour Dough

This dough is very pliable, and it rarely cracks when drying. Flour Dough can be braided, pressed through a garlic press, molded, and rolled—all with good results. The dough will, however, puff slightly while baking, which can provide interesting effects. If you want a colorful object, use food coloring or natural dyes before modelling. Or simply apply acrylic paints after drying. All objects made from Flour Dough should be sealed when dry if you want them to last. It's best to use clear acrylic spray, shellac, or varnish.

INGREDIENTS

4 cups (450 g) of flour
1 cup (225 g) of salt
1½ (350 ml) cups of water

DIRECTIONS

Stir all ingredients in a large mixing bowl.

Place the dough on a floured surface, and knead until it becomes smooth. If the dough is too stiff, add more water, a little at a time.

Store unused Flour Dough in a plastic bag in the refrigerator. It should keep indefinitely, but you may need to add more flour with each use.

To bake Flour Dough objects, place them on a foil-covered cookie sheet, and bake

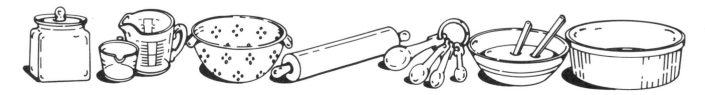

them at 300 degrees Fahrenheit (150 degrees Centigrade) until they're dry and hard. It will take 2 to 4 hours, depending on the size of the object(s) that you're baking.

Keep an eye on your baking. Over-dried objects will tend to be more fragile, and colors will not be as bright as those perfectly baked. Underbaked projects, on the other hand, will not keep well.

Salt Dough

This dough is heavy and very white, with a sparkling, shimmering look. Salt Dough can dry effectively at room temperature or in a warm oven. The finished dough projects will be extremely hard and durable when dry. If you wish, work food coloring, natural dyes, or water-based paint into the dough before modelling. Coloring Salt Dough creations *after* they dry will make the dough dull, instead of having its usual sparkle.

INGREDIENTS

2 cups (450 g) of salt
⅔ cup (155 ml) of water
1 cup (240 g) of cornstarch
½ cup (120 ml) of cold water
aluminum foil
cookie sheets

DIRECTIONS

Stir ⅔ cup (155 ml) of water and all the salt together in a saucepan over medium heat until it is well heated. Remove the pan from the stove.

Mix ½ cup (120 ml) of cold water and all the cornstarch together. Add the cornstarch mixture slowly to the salt mixture.

Return the pan to the stove, and cook the dough over medium heat until the mixture

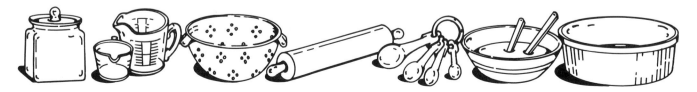

forms a soft ball. Remove the pan from the stove.

Put the dough on a foil-covered cookie sheet, and cover it with a damp cloth until it cools.

Shape objects on a foil-covered cookie sheet.

To dry Salt Dough objects, bake them in an oven at 200 degrees Fahrenheit (95 degrees Centigrade) for several hours. Or allow them to air-dry for 2 to 3 days.

Cornstarch Clay

This modelling clay works well for rolling-pin projects and small sculpted figures. It is easy to make and work with, but the clay will crack if it is overdried. So take care that you do not bake it too long. You can color the snow-white clay with food coloring or natural dyes before modelling. Or use acrylic paints after the objects dry thoroughly.

INGREDIENTS

2 cups (½ l) of baking soda
1 cup (240 g) of cornstarch
1¼ cups (300 ml) of cold water

DIRECTIONS

In a 2-quart saucepan, over low heat, mix baking soda and cornstarch. Add the water slowly while stirring to prevent lumps.

Cook the mixture for 6 minutes or until the mixture looks like mashed potatoes.

To cool, spread the dough on a cookie sheet, and cover it with a damp cloth.

Knead the dough for 10 minutes.

Store the clay dough in an airtight container when you're not using it. Bake Cornstarch Clay objects at 200 degrees Fahrenheit (95 degrees Centigrade) for 1½ to 3 hours. Cool and dry your creations completely—at least 24 hours.

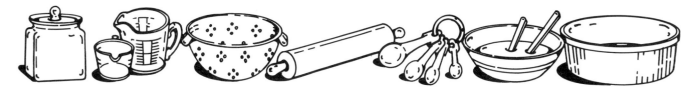

Soap Snow

It's fun to use Soap Snow to make snow sculptures, miniature snow forts, and indoor snowmen and snowwomen, but you can also create useful and decorative gift soaps with the same recipe.

INGREDIENTS

2 to 4 cups (32 to 64 T) of
   soap flakes
½ to 1 cup (120 to 235 ml) of water

DIRECTIONS

Begin with 2 cups (32 T) of soap flakes and ½ cup (120 ml) of water.

Use an electric mixer to whip the mixture until the "snow" becomes the consistency of cookie dough.

Add more flakes and water, as needed.

GIFT SOAPS

To make gift soaps, you can sculpt interesting shapes, then let the Soap Snow item dry completely. If you use cookie cutters, pat the Soap Snow into a thick "sheet" (like rolled cookie dough) on waxed paper or plastic wrap. Then cut out the shapes and allow them to dry. You can also press Soap Snow into candy and cookie molds, then turn onto a surface covered with waxed paper to dry. When the soaps are completely dry, wrap Soap Snow gift soaps individually in tissue paper or plastic wrap.

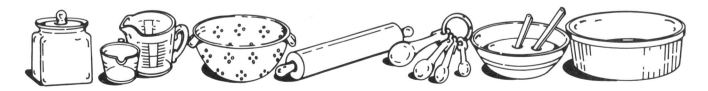

Sugar Cookies

INGREDIENTS

1 stick (8 tablespoons or 112 g) of
    butter or margarine
½ cup (125 g) of sugar
2 eggs

1 teaspoon (5 ml) of vanilla
½ teaspoon (2.5 ml) of almond flavor-
    ing (optional)
2 teaspoons (10 ml) of baking
    powder
2½ cups (312 g) of flour

★ ★ ★ ★ ★ ★ ★

DIRECTIONS

Blend the margarine and sugar until it
becomes light and fluffy. Use an electric
mixer for this part, if you wish.

Add the eggs, vanilla, and almond flavor-
ing. Beat well.

Add the baking powder and flour, and mix
until the dough forms a ball. The dough
will be very stiff.

Wrap the dough in plastic, and refrigerate
it at least 1 hour before rolling and cutting
or shaping it. This unbaked dough can be
used for Lollipop Cookies (see p. 52).

Roll out the dough to ¼ inch (6 mm) thick.
Use cookie cutters or form the dough into
desired shapes.

With a spatula, place the cookies on a
greased cookie sheet. Bake in a preheated

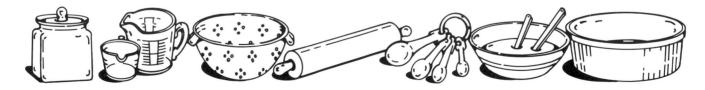

oven at 350 degrees Fahrenheit (175 degrees Centigrade) for 10 to 12 minutes or until done.

With this basic recipe you can invent many cookie variations. Make cookie lollipops, top with a frosting glaze, or add nuts, chocolate chips, or gumdrops. Experiment to see what suits your taste buds.

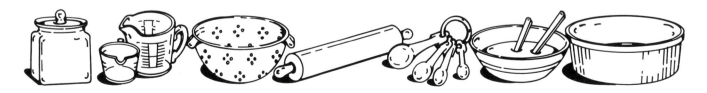

Chocolate Drop Pops

INGREDIENTS

½ cup (115 g) of shortening
1 cup (250 g) of sugar
1 egg
¾ cup (180 ml) of milk
1 teaspoon (5 ml) of vanilla
1¾ cups (225 g) of flour

½ cup (100 g) of unsweetened cocoa
  powder
½ teaspoon (2.5 ml) of baking soda
½ teaspoon (2.5 ml) of salt

FOR DECORATION

1 cup (170 g) of chocolate chips
colored candy sprinkles

★ ★ ★ ★ ★ ★ ★

DIRECTIONS

With mixer, blend the shortening, sugar, and egg until creamy. Add milk and vanilla, and beat well.

Stir together the flour, cocoa, baking soda, and salt; then beat into the sugar and shortening mixture until the dough is smooth. Drop a heaping teaspoon of dough onto a lightly greased cookie sheet.

Place a clean Popsicle stick in the middle of the dropped dough, pressing the stick lightly into the middle, but not all the way to the bottom, of the cookie sheet.

Place a small glob of dough on top of the exposed Popsicle stick.

Repeat this process until the dough is gone, leaving plenty of space between each cookie. Eight cookies and sticks fit nicely on an average-size baking sheet.

Bake in preheated oven at 350 degrees Fahrenheit (175 degrees Centigrade) for 8 to 12 minutes, until done.

Cool, and remove the cookies from the pan carefully with a spatula.

TO DECORATE

Place 1 cup of chocolate chips in a microwavable bowl, and microwave on high for 1 to 3 minutes, stirring frequently. Don't overcook!

When the chips are just melted, drizzle the chip frosting with a spoon onto the top of the cookie pop, then sprinkle the cookie with colored candy sprinkles.

Fast & Fabulous Frosting Glaze

This delicious stuff is not as thick as frosting or as runny as a glaze. It's easy for both kids and adults to use.

INGREDIENTS

2 tablespoons (35 g) of butter or margarine

1½ cups (250 g) of confectioners' sugar

1 to 3 tablespoons (15 to 45 ml) of milk

1 teaspoon (5 ml) of vanilla extract

½ teaspoon (2.5 ml) of almond extract

DIRECTIONS

Melt the butter, and place it in a small bowl. Add the confectioners' sugar and blend. Add the milk to the sugar, 1 tablespoon (15 ml) at a time, beating until the frosting is thick enough to drop slowly from a spoon. Add the vanilla and almond extracts and beat well.

When you use the frosting glaze, a thin "crust" may form on the top. Stir the frosting regularly in the bowl while you are applying it.

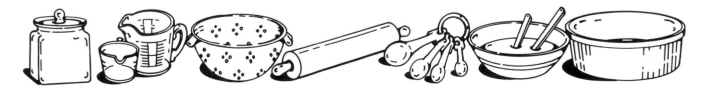

Crunchy Creature Stew

INGREDIENTS

1 cup (250 g) of peanut butter
1 to 2 cups (300 to 600 g) of sun-
  flower seeds or wild birdseed

½ cup (125 g) of raisins or cranberries (optional)
½ cup (150 g) of peanuts or other
  nuts (optional)

DIRECTIONS

Melt the peanut butter in a large bowl in a microwave, or melt the peanut butter slowly in a pan on the stove. Remove the pan from the heat, and stir in the rest of the ingredients until they're coated with peanut butter.

Adding different ingredients to the basic stew recipe will attract a variety of wild creatures. Bits of bacon or suet will attract woodpeckers. Finches and other songbirds favor thistle seed. Chickadees, jays, and squirrels love peanuts and walnuts.

Since Crunchy Creature Stew is quite sticky, you can smear leftovers directly onto tree trunks, branches, and stumps. All kinds of winged and four-footed creatures will invite themselves to dine in your yard.

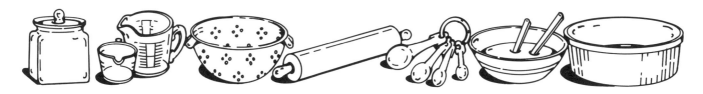

Potpourri

Potpourri is a mixture of flower petals, spices, herbs, and scented oils which, when dried, create a pleasant smell. Potpourri can be used loose in baskets or jars, as air fresheners, or stuffed into tiny pillows for sachets. Try experimenting with a variety of flowers, spices, and oils to find the scents you like best. Most of the ingredients for potpourris can be found in the spice section of grocery stores, in craft shops, in your own kitchen, and in backyard gardens.

SUGGESTED INGREDIENTS

Bases
rose petals
lavender blossoms
peppermint leaves
geranium petals
peel from lemons, limes, oranges,
   and tangerines

Fixative
orrisroot

Spices
allspice
cinnamon
nutmeg
cloves
ginger
mace

Oils
lemon and orange oils
rose oil
perfume

MAKING POTPOURRI

1. Choose one or more ingredients from *each* of the four groups above—bases, spices, oils, and fixative(s). Let your nose decide which fragrances blend nicely.

2. Dry the flower petals and citrus peels. Place them in single layers on paper towels and allow them to air-dry, which may take from several days to weeks. Or place the petals and peels in a single layer on paper towels and process them in a microwave oven for 3 to 5 minutes on MEDIUM. If you air-dry the petals and peels, replace the paper towels daily. Turn the petals and peels over to speed their drying and prevent them from becoming moldy. For your potpourri, these petals and peels should be *very* dry, like brown fall leaves that easily crumble.

3. In a large bowl, mix several cups of the flower petals or citrus peels, 1 to 2 tablespoons (15 to 30 ml) of each of your chosen spice(s), 6 to 10 drops of *one* oil, and 2 teaspoons (10 ml) of orrisroot.

Your potpourri is ready to use. Find a small container or basket to hold your sweet concoction, or sew tiny sachets or pillows for it. Sachets add a nice fragrance to closets and drawers—and to the clothes kept inside.

Natural Dyes & Inks

In early times, people used berries, leaves, roots, and herbs to add color to various everyday objects. They also used these natural objects to paint both face and body. It's probably *not* a good idea to dye *yourself* since colors borrowed from nature often stain, and some natural dyes are harmful to your skin. But it's fun making your own paints and inks for drawings and other painted objects from things found in nature. These finished colors may not be as bright as many store-bought products colored with synthetic chemicals, but why not experiment? You can work with color just as ancient peoples once did.

NATURAL OBJECTS THAT STAIN

Berries   Berries offer a variety of color possibilities. Gather them from fields and forests or buy them from the grocery store. Try raspberries, blueberries, blackberries, and a wide assortment of inedible berries.

Leaves and grasses   The kind of leaf or grass you collect will determine the color of your dye. Thick green leaves will produce more vivid colors than thinner leaves. However, freshly cut grass works well, too.

Kitchen spices   Try cinnamon sticks, powdered cinnamon, and ginger root.

Flower petals Blossoms from dandelions, zinnias, day lilies, and tulips are good choices for making dyes, and the colors created from begonia blossoms are especially vibrant.

Tree bark Experiment with barks from different trees to discover subtle differences in the colors produced.

Thick tree roots and dried bulbs The roots of dead trees and dried flower bulbs create unusual colors, depending on the type of tree or bulb used. These colors will not be bright, but they will produce authentic colors used long ago.

Vegetables and vegetable skins Many vegetables, like carrots, beets and spinach, which you may have in your home garden, make lovely ink and dye colors. The peels from potatoes, zucchini, and onions are just a few of the kinds of vegetable skin which produce natural colors.

MAKING NATURAL DYES & INKS

Chop all your berries, leaves, grasses, or other natural objects as finely as possible, and place them in a saucepan for the stove or in a glass or ceramic bowl for a microwave.

Add enough water to completely cover the objects.

On the stove, bring the water to a boil in the saucepan, then allow it to simmer for 15 to 30 minutes. If necessary, add more water, a little at a time. If you use a microwave, heat the items in the bowl on HIGH for

3 to 8 minutes—until the water turns the color you want.

Cooking times will vary, depending on the number and quality of the items you are using. You'll probably want to experiment with cooking time, amount of water, and the number of natural objects used for dyes to produce the effect you desire. Trial and error is how our ancient forebears learned, too!

Don't expect natural inks and dyes to be as vivid as synthetic inks and dyes. To produce brighter natural colors, increase the amount of petals, roots, leaves, berries, blossoms, bark, skins, grounds, grasses, or vegetables, and combine them with a small amount of water. Cook slowly for a longer period, stirring frequently.

CREATING SPECIFIC COLORS

Brown roots, bark, coffee grounds, tea bags

Red cranberries, beets, raspberries, bright-red wild berries

Blue blueberries, chopped red cabbage, red onion skins

Green grass clippings, green leaves, parsley, spinach, moss

Yellow flower blossoms—yellow marigolds, daffodils, yellow onion skins

Purple blackberries, purple plums, purple flower blossoms

Orange combine yellow and red dyes, or use carrots

USES FOR NATURAL DYES

Dye fabrics and yarns.

Stain everyday objects.

Use them as a substitute for water-color paints.

Dye eggshells. Only use dyes made from *edible* substances, if you plan to eat the eggs inside.

Create stamping ink.

Color homemade craft doughs, like the Salt Dough, Flour Dough, or Cornstarch Clay.

Stamp Pads

You can buy stamp pads filled with ink from craft, variety, and office supply stores. These pads will work well with your own roller printers and with small, handmade printing blocks. You can also make your own stamp pads. It's fairly easy.

YOU'LL NEED

small sponge for each color
container slightly larger than the
    sponge with a tightly fitting lid
paint, bottled ink, or natural dye

DIRECTIONS

Place the sponge in the container bowl, and saturate it with the colored paint, ink, or dye. Avoid over-saturating the pad, or you'll just get a puddle in the bottom of the bowl. In fact, if the sponge is not very wet, the printer will work better, and the paper on which you print will dry more quickly.

When the stamp pad is not in use, secure the container's lid, and store it in a cool place. If you use natural materials for the dye, store the pad in the refrigerator to reduce mold growth. If you do not use the ink pad for a long time, you may need to add a few drops of water or paint to the sponge to make it wet once more.

About Paints & Inks

Acrylics   Acrylic paints work well on porous surfaces, like things made out of doughs and clays. You'll find acrylics in tubes and jars in variety stores and craft shops. It's OK to thin these paints with water for water-color painting, but they work best on homemade crafts when you add little or no water.

Fabric Paints   There is a wide variety of paints available in craft and sewing stores which work well with fabrics. Some of these fabric paints come in tubes or bottles with narrow tips for writing words and making fine line designs. Others are specifically for splatter-painting or tie-dyeing. You'll find sparkly paints and glow-in-the-dark paints, too. And the best thing about many of these products is they are easy to use and machine-washable.

If you want to get creative with these paints, you can smear the colors on your fabric using small pieces of cardboard as "paintbrushes." Or dip cardboard shapes into some squeezed-out paint and press onto the fabric. Lift carefully to prevent smearing the design.

Let painted items dry flat for 12 to 24 hours before using. And wait at least 3 days before laundering. Machine drying is not recommended.

Food Coloring Mix 1 teaspoon (5 ml) of vinegar for each ½ cup (120 ml) of water, and food coloring will perform as a dye. But be careful: colors can bleed and fade when laundered. Also try food coloring for printing with blocks and rollers.

Ink Bottled ink is available in a variety of colors. You can buy it at office supply or variety stores. Use these inks for painting nonporous surfaces as well as for block and roller printing. You can also find ready-to-use stamp pads in many colors. Also look for rainbow stamp pads that include several colors in a single pad.

Natural Dyes and Paints Made from substances found in nature, these dyes and paints provide unusual color options for craft projects.

Most colors created from natural materials will not turn out as vivid as synthetic colors. However, these dyes offer subtle tones, and they allow lots of creativity.

Tempera This water-based paint can be used wherever watercolors might be used. Tempera comes in powdered form as well as liquid form, and is available in variety, craft, and art stores.

Watercolors Watercolor paints are available in most stores, and they're inexpensive. They work best on less porous surfaces. Avoid using them on most homemade dough creations, since the moisture will soften the finished product. When mixed with small amounts of water, watercolors can be used to color eggshells. But only use them if you remove the egg before coloring.

Money-Making Ideas

Many of the projects described in this book are suitable for gift-giving, but you can also create items to sell. At some arts and crafts fairs, tables are reserved for selling items that are hand-made by children. If a neighbor is having a garage sale, you might be allowed to display and sell your crafts. Or how about inviting your young friends to help you organize a neighborhood kids' crafts sale? You'll need a special permit and the help of an adult to sell your crafts at a shopping center or mall, so don't set up a table in these locations (or on the street) without getting permission first. The following projects described in this book make both lovely gift and sale items.

Blizzard in a Jar

To make this snow globe more attractive for selling, cover the lid with a circle of fabric cut with pinking shears, then tie a ribbon around the place where the lid and jar meet.

Roller Printing

Bundle printed note cards together in groups of four or six and wrap them in see-through sandwich bags. Be sure to size the cards so that they will fit store-bought envelopes, and include an envelope for each note card.

Hobbyhorse Puppets

Rather than selling these stuffed ponies, sell tickets to a puppet play you and your friends write and produce. The hobbyhorse ponies will be the characters!

Crayon Batik

Priced individually, these Helping Hands dish towels will be popular.

Bookmark Corners

These can be an inexpensive item for kids to purchase with allowance money.

Block Printing

Try purchasing postcards which do not have pictures on the front. Office supply shops and your local post office may have these available. Then you can sell decorated postcards. Sell them individually or packaged like the roller-print note cards. Don't forget to add the cost of the postcard to your selling price.

Lollipop Cookies

Home-baked foods are always a hit at craft sales. Wrap each lollipop cookie separately in plastic wrap so that it will stay fresh and clean before the sale.

Sand-Castle Candles

When pricing your candles (and other sale items), figure your cost in making the product and then add a *fair* amount for your labor to the final price tag.

Gift Soaps

Use the Soap Snow recipe (p. 107) found in the Recipe File to craft decorative soaps for sale.

Pinecone Flowers

Sell these delicate "flowers" individually or in groups of three or five.

Yarn Flowers

Gather six matching flowers or flowers with coordinating colors. Tie small bunches together with a ribbon.

Wishing Pin

Keep the price low on these pins so that they are attainable by all who dare to dream of wishes-come-true.

Tin-Punch Pictures

Make holiday designs and all-occasion designs to satisfy the interests and needs of all shoppers.

Pinecone Creature Feeders

Nature lovers everywhere will flock to your table to purchase this treat for their feathered and furry friends.

Tooth-Fairy Pockets

Here's another inexpensive item for very young shoppers. While they wait, you can even personalize the pocket with the child's name. Try using a fine-line permanent marker or laundry marker.

Mosaic Medallions

Craft these with care and attention to detail, then add high-quality ribbons for the neck chain.

Burlap Baskets

To help shoppers see the versatility of these baskets, display several of them filled with your handmade flowers or Potpourri. You could even sell Potpourri, Dried Flowers, or Yarn Flowers along with them.

Baked Napkin Rings

To show off these popular items nicely, pull a pretty linen napkin through one ring, and place it on a coordinating place mat.

Index

Metric Equivalents

Inches

Millimetres

Centimetres